Negroes
with
Guns

by
ROBERT F. WILLIAMS

Edited by Marc Schleifer

www.bnpublishing.com

info@bnpublishing.com

For information regarding special discounts for bulk purchases, please contact
BN Publishing at

sales@bnpublishing.com

TABLE OF CONTENTS

EDITOR'S NOTE

It is eight years since the Supreme Court's historic decision on school segregation lifted the heart of the Negro people, giving strength to the struggle for voting rights and for integration of public facilities. The tenacious resistance of Southern racists including the use of violence condoned, when not abetted, by local authorities has given rise to bitter frustration and anger, bringing to the fore the issue of armed self-defense. In Monroe, North Carolina, under the leadership of Marine veteran Robert F. Williams, the Negro community took up guns for protection. Monroe, North Carolina has become the test case of the unqualified right of Negroes to armed self-defense when law and order break down.

The issue is biting deep in the Negro community and awareness of it is increasing in the rest of the country as symbolized by Jules Pfeiffer's cartoon in the *New York Post*, August 15, 1962. It is a portentous issue, being debated by articulate and thoughtful men, and we set forth here the position of the Reverend Martin Luther King, Jr. and that of the novelist and scholar on John Brown and the abolitionist movement, Truman Nelson, as an introduction to the story of the Monroe case by its central figure, Robert F. Williams.

Mr. Williams is now in Cuba, as a political exile. I was already there and obtained his story in a three-hour taped interview at the Hotel Capri, in the Vedado section of Havana (see photo opposite). The interview was broadcast by WBAI-FM in New York on May 31, 1962 and later by WKPF-FM, San Francisco. This book is essentially that interview, but to develop some of his points I've also used material from Mr. Williams' article and editorials in his newsletter, *The Crusader*, as well as from his interview with John Schultz published in *Studies on the Left*, Spring, 1962.

7

"HATE IS ALWAYS TRAGIC"

by Martin Luther King, Jr.

Those who adhere to the method of nonviolent direct action recognize that legislation and court orders tend only to declare rights; they can never thoroughly deliver them. Only when the people themselves begin to act are rights on paper given lifeblood. The method of nonviolent resistance is effective in that it has a way of disarming the opponent; it exposes his moral defenses, it weakens his morale and at the same time it works on his conscience.

Nonviolent resistance also provides a creative force through which men can channelize their discontent. It does not require that they abandon their discontent. This discontent is sound and healthy. Nonviolence saves it from degenerating into morbid bitterness and hatred. Hate is always tragic. It is as injurious to the hater as it is to the hated. It distorts the personality and scars the soul. Psychiatrists are telling us now that many of the inner conflicts and strange things that happen in the subconscious are rooted in hate. So they are now saying, "Love or perish." This is the beauty of nonviolence. It says you can struggle without hating; you can fight war without violence.

As a race, we must work passionately and unrelentingly for first-class citizenship, but we must never use second-class methods to gain it. If this happens, unborn generations will be the recipients of a long and desolate night of bitterness, and our chief legacy to the future will be an endless reign of meaningless chaos.

We have come to the day when a piece of freedom is not enough for us as human beings nor for the nation of which we are part. We have been given pieces, but unlike bread, a slice of which does diminish hunger, a piece of liberty no longer suffices. Freedom is like life. You cannot

9

be given life in installments. You cannot be given breath but not body, nor a heart but no blood vessels. Freedom is one thing—you have it all, or you are not free.

Our destiny is bound up with the destiny of America— we built it for two centuries without wages, we made cotton king, we built our homes and homes for our masters and suffered injustice and humiliation, but out of a bottomless vitality continued to live and grow. If the inexpressible cruelties of slavery could not extinguish our existence, the opposition we now face will surely fail. We feel that we are the conscience of America—we are its troubled soul.

(from an address to the National Press Club, Washington, D.C., July, 1962)

THE SOCIAL ORGANIZATION OF NON-VIOLENCE

by *Martin Luther King, Jr.*

Paradoxically, the struggle for civil rights has reached a stage of profound crisis, although its outward aspect is distinctly less turbulent and victories of token integration have been won in the hard-resistance areas of Virginia and Arkansas.

The crisis has its origin in a decision rendered by the Supreme Court more than a year ago, which upheld the pupil placement law. Though little noticed then, this decision fundamentally weakened the historic 1954 ruling of the Court. It is imperceptibly becoming the basis of a *de facto* compromise between the powerful contending forces.

The 1954 decision required for effective implementation resolute Federal action supported by mass action to undergird all necessary changes. It is obvious that Federal action by the legislative and executive branches was half-hearted and inadequate. The activity of Negro forces, while heroic in some instances, and impressive in other sporadic situations, lacked consistency and militancy sufficient to fill the void left by government default. The segregationists were swift to seize these advantages, and unrestrained by moral or social conscience, defied the law boldly and brazenly.

The net effect of this social equation has led to the present situation, which is without clear-cut victory for either side. Token integration is a developing pattern. This type of integration is merely an affirmation of a principle without the substance of change.

It is, like the Supreme Court decision, a pronouncement of justice, but by itself does not insure that the millions

11

of Negro children will be educated in conditions of equality. This is not to say that it is without value. It has substantial importance. However, it fundamentally changes the outlook of the whole movement, for it raises the prospect of long, slow change without a predictable end. As we have seen in Northern cities, token integration has become a pattern in many communities and remained frozen, even though environmental attitudes are substantially less hostile to full integration than in the South.

This then is the danger. Full integration can easily become a distant or mythical goal—major integration may be long postponed, and in the quest for social calm a compromise firmly implanted in which the real goals are merely token integration for a long period to come.

The Negro was the tragic victim of another compromise in 1878, when his full equality was bargained away by the Federal Government and a condition somewhat above slave status but short of genuine citizenship became his social and political existence for nearly a century.

There is reason to believe that the Negro of 1959 will not accept supinely any such compromises in the contemporary struggle for integration. His struggle will continue, but the obstacles will determine its specific nature. It is axiomatic in social life that the imposition of frustrations leads to two kinds of reactions. One is the development of a wholesome social organization to resist with effective, firm measures any efforts to impede progress. The other is a confused, anger-motivated drive to strike back violently, to inflict damage. Primarily, it seeks to cause injury to retaliate for wrongful suffering. Secondarily, it seeks real progress. It is punitive—not radical or constructive.

The current calls for violence have their roots in this latter tendency. Here one must be clear that there are three different views on the subject of violence. One is the approach of pure nonviolence, which cannot readily or

12

easily attract large masses, for it requires extraordinary discipline and courage. The second is violence exercised in self-defense, which all societies from the most primitive to the most cultured and civilized, accept as moral and legal. The principle of self-defense, even involving weapons and bloodshed, has never been condemned, even by Gandhi, who sanctioned it for those unable to master pure nonviolence. The third is the advocacy of violence as a tool of advancement, organized as in warfare, deliberately and consciously. To this tendency many Negroes are being tempted today. There are incalculable perils in this approach. It is not the danger or sacrifice of physical being which is primary, though it cannot be contemplated without a sense of deep concern for human life. The greatest danger is that it will fail to attract Negroes to a real collective struggle, and will confuse the large uncommitted middle group, which as yet has not supported either side. Further, it will mislead Negroes into the belief that this is the only path and place them as a minority in a position where they confront a far larger adversary than it is possible to defeat in this form of combat. When the Negro uses force in self-defense he does not forfeit support—he may even win it, by the courage and self-respect it reflects. When he seeks to initiate violence he provokes questions about the necessity for it, and inevitably is blamed for its consequences. It is unfortunately true that however the Negro acts, his struggle will not be free of violence initiated by his enemies, and he will need ample courage and willingness to sacrifice to defeat this manifestation of violence. But if he seeks it and organizes it, he cannot win. Does this leave the Negro without a positive method to advance? Mr. Robert Williams would have us believe that there is no collective and practical alternative. He argues that we must be cringing and submissive or take up arms. To so place the issue distorts the whole problem. There are other meaningful alternatives.

The Negro people can organize socially to initiate many forms of struggle which can drive their enemies back without resort to futile and harmful violence. In the history of the movement for racial advancement, many creative forms have been developed—the mass boycott, sitdown protests and strikes, sit-ins,—refusal to pay fines and bail for unjust arrests—mass marches—mass meetings—prayer pilgrimages, etc. Indeed, in Mr. Williams' own community of Monroe, North Carolina, a striking example of collective community action won a significant victory without use of arms or threats of violence. When the police incarcerated a Negro doctor unjustly, the aroused people of Monroe marched to the police station, crowded into its halls and corridors, and refused to leave until their colleague was released. Unable to arrest everyone, the authorities released the doctor and neither side attempted to unleash violence. This experience was related by the doctor who was the intended victim.

There is more power in socially organized masses on the march than there is in guns in the hands of a few desperate men. Our enemies would prefer to deal with a small armed group rather than with a huge, unarmed but resolute mass of people. However, it is necessary that the mass-action method be persistent and unyielding. Gandhi said the Indian people must "never let them rest," referring to the British. He urged them to keep protesting daily and weekly, in a variety of ways. This method inspired and organized the Indian masses and disorganized and demobilized the British. It educates its myriad participants, socially and morally. All history teaches us that like a turbulent ocean beating great cliffs into fragments of rock, the determined movement of people incessantly demanding their rights always disintegrates the old order.

It is this form of struggle—non-cooperation with evil through mass actions—"never letting them rest"—which offers the more effective road for those who have been tempted and goaded to violence. It needs the bold and the

14

brave because it is not free of danger. It faces the vicious and evil enemies squarely. It requires dedicated people, because it is a backbreaking task to arouse, to organize, and to educate tens of thousands for disciplined, sustained action. From this form of struggle more emerges that is permanent and damaging to the enemy than from a few acts of organized violence.

Our present urgent necessity is to cease our internal fighting and turn outward to the enemy, using every form of mass action yet known—create new forms—and resolve never to let them rest. This is the social lever which will force open the door to freedom. Our powerful weapons are the voices, the feet, and the bodies of dedicated, united people, moving without rest toward a just goal. Greater tyrants than Southern segregationists have been subdued and defeated by this form of struggle. We have not yet used it, and it would be tragic if we spurn it because we have failed to perceive its dynamic strength and power.

To set the record straight on any implications that I am inconsistent in my struggle against war and too weak-kneed to protest nuclear war, may I state that repeatedly, in public addresses and in my writings, I have unequivocally declared my hatred for this most colossal of all evils and I have condemned any organizer of war, regardless of his rank and nationality. I have signed numerous statements with other Americans condemning nuclear testing and have authorized publication of my name in advertisements appearing in the largest circulation newspapers in the country, without concern that it was then "unpopular" to so speak out.

(*Liberation, October,* 1959)

THE RESISTANT SPIRIT

by Truman Nelson

The real test of a leader is whether he is prophetical: whether he has impacted in him those elements which, once accepted in his image, can transform many people completely, and millions of others to a point where they can accept this transformation without active resistance. The revolution within the law—the keeping of the law when the government breaks it—now taking place in the South has cast up two leaders. Both, fortunately and inevitably, are Negroes and they have both given their total concern to the complete liberation of their people.

One, Martin Luther King, is popular, highly regarded by the press and considered above reproach in liberal and genuinely religious circles. He is an eloquent man and has ready access to almost all national media, infinitely more than any of his race has ever had before (a great achievement in itself); his passage in and out of Southern jails has become almost a national sabbatical observance, well illustrated by every form of picture making. His prayers and protestations of love for his enemies, his dignity, the appealing power of his serious, intact personality, the overwhelming invulnerability of his moral position seemingly leave nothing to be desired in him but the stamina to last out, in his person, a struggle which he constantly compares to Gandhi's forty-year effort to free India.

The other, Robert Williams, is almost exactly the reverse of this. He is either completely ignored or viciously attacked by the press. His image now luridly persists in circulars in post offices all over the country as a fugitive from justice, a "wanted" man. He is described as "heavily armed and dangerous," and as a madman, a schizophrenic. He is said to be in unlawful flight to avoid prosecution for kid-

Robert F. Williams (photo by LeRoy McLucas).

napping; citizens are urged to inform the F.B.I. of his whereabouts. No official has seen fit to take down this vindictive circular, this printed form of character assassination, although it has been known for many, many months that Williams is a political refugee in Cuba. Furthermore, the alleged "kidnapping" for which he was hunted with drawn guns is of such little moment that others under the identical indictment, and in the law's custody right now, have not been brought to trial a year after the incident, and the trial has now been adjourned, *sine die!*

If anyone on the American scene would seem to be a "damaged soul," it is this harried man, whose life has been one of constant struggle and flight, who is in exile, whose personality has been placed in some sort of awful limbo in the American consciousness as having lost all value for the struggle to which he pledged his existence long ago. And yet there is a nagging doubt in many people whether Williams is not the real prophet of the two.

It is possible to appease this doubt by saying, well, they are both prophets, both useful, each in his own way, but somehow history does not permit this plural vision of redemptive personalities. It is either/or when the chips are down, and history has a curious way of selecting the most unlikely and unloved people for its charismatic figures. I must confess that it is the sheer "orneriness" of Williams that catches my eye, my attention, and my profound sympathy. The fact that he is kept out of the press, that he is difficult, that he cannot adjust himself to loving his enemies, that he is almost always vituperous and undiplomatic toward the political rulers of the South and has made implacable enemies of them all, from the Governor of his state, who calls full-dress news conferences to denounce him, down to the chief and the rest of the police force of Monroe, North Carolina, who call him on the phone to tell him he will be hanging in the square before the courthouse in a few minutes . . . this makes me hear in him the thunder of Sinai.

But the question cannot be settled merely by saying Williams has the sound of the prophet, as precisely as the ring of silver on marble. The saint must be given his due. Martin Luther King has made great advances in a cause to which his own devotion has been unsurpassed. He has a clear posture of advance, and it has worked before and may again. His management of the Montgomery bus boycott, in which he exploited the technique of non-cooperation with evil through mass action, brought the attention of the world to the Negro plight. Furthermore, he won; the buses are no longer segregated in Montgomery, Alabama. And he won in a peaceful way, while under brutal attack, not excluding attempts to take his life. During it all, in spite of provocation of the most exacerbating kind, he never lost control of his policy of non-violent resistance.

However, the current application of these techniques in Albany, Georgia, while evoking stupendous publicity, has not been effective in achieving Negro demands for racial equality there. If the Albany Movement is a benchmark of massive desegregation, than it indicates stalemate, or regression. To many, it is King's methods that are at fault here and it is appropriate to let them pass once more in review.

Martin Luther King has developed a line of strategy now so widely accepted that there is a danger that he will become the present-day Booker T. Washington, and will have to be dealt with, ultimately, as a positive hindrance to Negro liberation. Already, liberals are cataloging as "good" Negroes and "bad" Negroes those who, respectively, follow King or Robert Williams. The editor of a leading New York liberal newspaper, asked recently why he did not tell the full story of Williams and Monroe, visibly retreated, saying: Williams is a bad guy.

There are many points of divergence between these two. One, mentioned as a gambit, is that King does not make allowance for, or establish protection against, reprisals, as

Williams does. The importance of this maneuver can be swiftly taught by this news story out of Albany, Georgia:

"A week after the Negro college students' prayer for freedom, six carloads of men broke into the house of one of the students and, armed with guns, clubs and iron pipes, beat the boy and his mother and sister. The mother's leg was broken, her scalp smashed open, and her hands crushed, and she spent three months on crutches. In a sworn statement, she said that one of the men who had beaten her was a police deputy. No charges were lodged."

Williams says that this kind of incident would not have happened in Monroe after the Negroes armed there, because they were "people with strength."

There has been a certain amount of debate between King and Williams. It has not been very intense because the Negro people are wiser than we are, and do not destroy one another out of doctrinal differences. Both make concessions of agreement with the correctness of the other's position. King says that the principle of self-defense, even involving weapons and bloodshed, "has never been condemned, even by Gandhi, who sanctioned it for those *unable to master pure non-violence.*" The inference here is that somewhat inferior people defend themselves violently but allowance must be made for their human imperfection . . . or lack of theological school training.

Williams, in this very book, says he is not against the passive resistance advocated by King and others, but differs with him only over the lack of flexibility pacifist commitments impose on a struggle. At other times, however, Williams has made serious charges which should be further ventilated. He claims that hundreds of thousands of dollars are being sent into the South to convert the Negroes into non-violence, to buy the militancy out of them, and thereby to prolong the very condition of passivity to wrong which he feels brought on the brutal exploitation of the Negro in the first place. He says the Uncle Toms of the South are the most outspoken exponents of non-violence,

20

and profit most from the form the struggle is presently taking.

King, although giving lip service to support of Williams, constantly refers to everything but non-violent resistance as a "second-class method." This does not seem to me very helpful to the Williams school of resistance. Furthermore, it never fails to infuriate me personally as a form of segregation in itself—making me, for example, of the second class because I cannot, temperamentally or historically, accept the validity of total passive resistance. It makes me want to lock horns with King, to debate him.

As the heir of a great tradition of revolutionary morality, I resent his position, not believing that Lexington Green, Concord Bridge, and the celebration of the Fourth of July were at all second class. This second class-ship is extendable to the great resistance movements of World War II against the Nazis. It can be extended to various phases of the African struggle, to the liberation now shaping up in Angola and just consummated in Algeria.

It is, in fact, so utterly inconsistent with our American tradition and what I believe is still basic in the hearts and minds of the American people as a whole that I think it should be attacked as an error, a damaging heresy, and that Mr. King should debate the whole question with someone outside his own race, and so let the chips fall where they may. And speaking of race, I might also say that I believe that the non-violent resistance advocated by Mr. King is acceptable to vast numbers of whites in this country because it is racist.

William Lloyd Garrison, the only truly creative American pacifist, was so strongly of this opinion that he would not tolerate anyone denying the slave weapons of force and insurrection without denying himself, all other whites, his government and every other government in the world the same advantage, and held that as long as there was a tool of coercion in the hands of anyone, only a pure pacifist and anarchist could deny a like weapon to the slave.

21

His vehemence and rancor on this question come out fully in his review of *Uncle Tom's Cabin*:

"That all slaves of the South ought to repudiate all carnal weapons, shed no blood, be obedient to their masters, wait for peaceful deliverance and abstain from all insurrectionary movements is everywhere taken for granted, because the *victims are black!* They cannot return blow for blow, or conspire for the destruction of their oppressors. *They* are required by the Bible to put away all wrath, to submit to every conceivable outrage without resistance. None of *their* advocates may seek to inspire them to imitate the example of the Greeks, the Poles, the Hungarians, our revolutionary sires, for such teaching would evince a most un-Christian and blood-thirsty disposition. But for those whose skin is of a different complexion, the case is materially altered. Talk not to the whites of peacefully submitting, of overcoming evil with good when they are spit upon and buffeted, outraged and oppressed. . . . Oh No, for them it is, let the blood of the tyrants flow! Is there one law of submission for the black man and another law of rebellion and conflict for the white man? When it is that the whites are trodden in the dust, does Christ justify them in taking up arms to vindicate their rights? And when it is the blacks that are thus treated, does Christ require them to be patient, long suffering, harmless and forgiving?"

Martin Luther King's theoretical position is supposed to be half Christ, half Gandhi, but the Christian line is hardly applicable to the avowed militancy of non-violent active resistance. The appropriate Bible text says quite clearly to "Resist not evil but whosoever shall smite thee on the right cheek, turn to him the other also." It takes considerable manipulation to say that this means "Do resist evil." King states emphatically in his *Stride Toward Freedom* that non-violent resistance is true resistance and "ultimately the way of the strong man." That is to say, it is "passive physically," but strongly active "spiritually." I must confess that Dr. King and myself part company right here. I can-

22

not conceive how anyone can resist an assailant "spiritually" unless it is possible to interrupt a headlong rush of assault by some sort of instant hypnosis.

He mentions several other precepts of Gandhi which I find highly debatable. One does not seek to defeat, for example, one's opponent or humiliate him in any way so that one creates, after the struggle, "the beloved community." Nor does one apply condemnation of the evil being attacked to any specific person. The basic tension in the South, he says, is not between white people and Negro people but between justice and injustice. By loving them, he feels that the Southern whites will see that their side is one of injustice and be awakened to a sense of moral shame which will bring, in the end, redemption and reconciliation.

It's going to be a long row to hoe to bring the white South to any sense of shame, or to make them wake up to the brute fact that the golden age they hark back to and are fighting tooth and nail to perpetuate was a slave-holding, slave-breeding, slave-driving, slave-hunting hell on earth. The crime of the white South is centered in their racist unity of loyalty which blinds them to the real state of their society and its discontents. I really do not think that their eyes will be opened by any words of love addressed to them by a people whom they have already trodden underfoot for hundreds of years, while saying all the while, that they loved *them* like their own families.

There is no question that King's method is permeated through and through with Gandhianism and that he has been striving with all his verbal might to fix it permanently in the minds of the struggling Negroes of the South. He quotes approvingly certain remarks of Gandhi which are as repulsive as any made by the most jingoistic of sword-rattling generals, calling for sacrifice and death. "Rivers of blood may have to flow before we gain our freedom, but it must be our blood," says Gandhi.

23

I find this utterly disgusting. Why should Gandhi, or any other human being, throw a whole people, bound and gagged against physical resistance, into the slaughter pen to submit and bleed until the slaughterer gets tired and puts off his killing clothes and goes about some other business, unpunished, even unquestioned, for his shedding of innocent blood. Who is Gandhi to decide whose blood is to be expendable?

Then King quotes Gandhi on willingness to go to jail if necessary, quotes him as saying one should go "as a Bridegroom enters the Bride's chamber." How ironic this is, and how naive! The young lad who goes into a Southern jail is actually more of a reluctant, terrified bride. There are perverts in these Southern jails; perverts, sadists, sexually corrupt men of unspeakable desires and violences.

These evil men are part of the penal apparatus of the white South. The beatings, kickings, and floggings, and other sexual indulgences they administer upon men sent among them for protesting racial injustices are approved by the authorities as part and parcel of the process of enforcement.

Not only are they approved, but prisoners are offered rewards for carrying them out . . . these obscene bargains. In Williams' own town of Monroe, Howard Stack, a pathologically violent man, in prison on assault charges, with a long record of this criminal activity, made a written confession that "The Monroe Police and deputy forces . . . put to me a proposition. If I would, by force, assault one of the Freedom Riders, they would see I went free of my charges."

Whereupon he beat one Richard Griswold nearly to death while the authorities turned their backs. This practice is apparently so inextricably connected with the forms of due process in the white South that, when appraised of it, and sent the handwritten confession, the Justice Department of the United States replied that it did not, in their eyes, reveal evidence of violation of a Federal law, and that they had closed their files on the whole matter.

24

The fact is that the real punishment, the *de facto* punishment of those arrested for protesting racist practices, comes during that confinement which King, quoting Gandhi, endorses as like a Bridegroom entering a Bride's chamber.

This is not to say that this cause is not worthy of going to jail for, but to candy this experience over with this saccharine rhetoric, so characteristic of this movement, prevents people from seeing the Southern jailhouses for what they really are—hell-holes of human degradation only slightly better than the Hitler death camps. Infernos where Freedom Riders, after the routine beatings by five or six deputies, have had their fingers bent back until they broke, their pants slashed and a high voltage electric cattle goad applied to their testicles. Where women have been whipped with wide leather belts on their bare breasts, buttocks, and between their legs, according to *The Catholic Worker*. Where, according to the *"50 States Report,"* a Government publication, people are killed before their trials by excesses of torture or jailhouse lynchings and reported as suicides. This is what Williams means whe he talks about the lack of flexibility in pacifist commitments. When you are pledged to love everybody and your adversary is a louse, how can you tell the truth about him?

One of the most disturbing aspects of the King line in respect to desegregation is that it does not relate closely to the historical struggle of abolitionism before the Civil War, a struggle which was truly integrated, and which worked. The quotations which follow represent in essence the line, the texts, the scriptures of the American Anti-Slavery Movement and it is obvious that the new testament that King is trying to build up out of Gandhianism does not evoke the same reverberations. Furthermore, it seems to me that the new texts of Martin Luther King are not rooted in the minds and hearts of the American people, and that in order for him to do this he will have to dislodge or gloss over some of the best outbursts of the high poetry of the resistant spirit.

The great abolitionist William Lloyd Garrison also called himself a non-resistant, and talked non-resistance. He told the slaves not to insurrect, but did so with the hard knowledge that if they did the Government of the United States would send an army against them in the name of the Union itself, and as part of the contract between the sections that slavery was to be tolerated and supported in return for Southern cooperation in the American Revolution.

Garrison felt that this immoral contract had to be broken first; this is why he had on the masthead of *The Liberator,* "No Union with Slaveholders. The U.S. Constitution is a covenant with death and an agreement with Hell." This grievous flaw in the Constitution was supposed to have been forever nullified by the Fourteenth Amendment but it is obvious that the accommodations it represented still hold in our national life in respect to the concessions made to Southern politicians defending Southern "institutions."

Garrison, in fact, began his career like King, saying that "moral suasion" would melt the hard hearts of the racist slaveholders, but he became disabused of this notion after a decade of futile effort. "There is not any instance recorded, either in sacred or profane history, in which the oppressors and enslavers of mankind, except in individual cases, have been induced by moral suasion, to surrender their despotic power and let the oppressed go free; but in nearly every instance, from the time that Pharaoh and his host were drowned in the Red Sea, down to the present day, they have persisted in their evil course until some sudden destruction came upon them, or they were compelled to surrender their ill gotten power in some other manner. Of all oppressors and tyrants who have cursed and afflicted mankind, none have ever equalled the enslavers of the colored race—especially American Republican Slaveholders—in ferociousness of spirit, moral turpitude of character, and desperate depravity of heart. I regard their conversion, as a body, to the side of bleeding humanity, by appeals to their understanding, consciences and hearts about as hopeless as any attempt to transform wolves and hyenas into lambs and doves by the same process. Their understandings have become brutish, their consciences seared as with a hot iron, and their hearts harder than adamant."

Garrison did not follow this up with an appeal for violence but he never stopped denouncing, with invective flowing like a stream of volcanic lava, the slaveholder, his family, and his whole society. He called them murderers, kidnappers, thieves, whoremongers, and used every incitement he could lay tongue to which would compel their expulsion from any connection with a democracy. Ideologically he hammered on a single point: the revolutionary contradictions that have been literally built into race relations in this land of the free. His age was then as full of revolutionary upheaval as ours is now (tremulous with light, he called it) and to those enthusiasts so eager to applaud the revolutions in Greece, France, and Hungary he suggested that the slaves "will find all the urgings and incentive to insurrect their want in your speeches, your parades, your celebrations. You do not regard anything done to a black man as an outrage, but touch your prerogatives and see how you threaten!"

As the Anti-Slavery Movement drew to its climax and the South found it necessary to use more and more Federal power to uphold its institutions, the men of conscience in the North were confronted with the issue of whether they would use violence against slavery and racism. It is one thing to say I have the courage not to resist in a Christlike way, any attack on my own person, but what if the man next to you is being brutally handled, and you have the means at hand to help him? Theodore Parker, in 1850, gave the answer of the decade to this dilemma.

In a meeting of the Boston ministers, a majority of them decided that the fugitive slave should be given up and the contract with the South adhered to; otherwise the nation would be rent unto destruction. Parker disagreed with this, instinctively and violently, saying:

"I would rather see my own house burnt to the ground, and my family thrown, one by one, amid the blazing rafters of my own roof, and I myself be thrown in last of all, rather than have a single fugitive slave sent back. I have in my church black men, fugitive slaves. They are the crown of my apostleship, the seal of my ministry. It becomes me to look after their bodies in order to save their souls. I have been obliged to take my own parishioners into my house to keep them out of the clutches of the kidnappers. I have had to arm myself. I have written my sermons with a pistol on my desk, loaded, a cap on the nipple and ready for action. Yea, with a drawn sword within reach of my right hand. This I have done in Boston; in the middle of the nineteenth century; have been obliged to do it to defend the members of my own church, women as well as men. You know I do not like fighting. I am no non-resistant; that nonsense never went down with me. But it is no small matter which will compel me to shed human blood. But what could I do? I was born in the little town where the fight and bloodshed of the Revolution began. The bones of the men who first fell in that war are covered by the monument at Lexington, it is 'sacred to liberty and the rights of mankind.' This is the first inscription that I ever read. These men are my kindred. My grandfather fired the first shot in the Revolution, the blood that flowed there was kindred to this which courses in my veins today. With these things before me, these symbols, with these memories, when a parishioner, a fugitive, pursued by kidnappers, came to my house, what could I do but take her in and defend her to the last? O, My brothers, I am not afraid of men. I can offend them, I care nothing for their hate, or their esteem. I am not very careful of my reputation. But I should not dare to violate the eternal law of God."

This, I submit, is a man speaking directly to the true American consciousness, the real, revolutionary American consciousness. This is how Americans think of themselves, this is what they admire and cleave to. This is the permanent in it, the noble in it, that which transcends the accidents in which politicians plunge us into unwitting support for tyrannies and corruptions. When the Negro is constantly presented to this consciousness as submissive, or passively resistant, or passive to attacks on his person, he is alien to it. It is alien to the Negro himself. I know he wants to resist and everyone else does too. But he is constantly being talked out of it and an image is superimposed over this will to resist, an image which the Southern racists want accepted, that the Negro will not fight for his own liberation, which is bad enough, but what is worse, will not turn a hand to save his brother, assaulted at his side. There may be a strengthening power of love in submitting to attack on yourself. But there is love as well in saving your brother, protecting him, fighting for him . . . one would think to hear the Gandhians talk that there is no love at all in laying down one's life for another.

This is the price, I feel, for full inclusion into the American consciousness, *the will to visibly resist*. Every great leader knew this. The miraculously transforming words of John Brown in his Speech to the Court were based on it. "Had I interfered in behalf of the rich, the powerful, the so-called great, or in behalf of any of their friends, either father, mother, brother, sister, wife or children, or any of that class, and suffered and sacrificed what I have in this interference, it would have been alright. Every man in this court would have deemed it an act worthy of reward rather than punishment."

No one has spoken more truly to the hearts of men meditating oppression, nor put men more movingly in the shoes of the oppressed. Even Garrison, still a pacifist-anarchist, could not deny its rightness. "I am a non-resistant—a believer in the inviolability of human life under all cir-

29

cumstances; I therefore, in the name of God, disarm John Brown and every slave at the South. But I do not stop here; if I did I would be a monster. I also disarm, in the name of God, every slaveholder and tyrant in the world. For wherever this principle is adopted, all fetters must instantly melt, and there can be no oppressed and no oppressor, in the nature of things. I not only desire, but have labored unceasingly to effect the peaceful abolition of slavery, by an appeal to the reason and conscience of every slaveholder; yet, as a peace man . . . an ultra peace man, I am prepared to say, success to every slave insurrection in the South and in every slave country. I do not see how I compromise or stain my peace profession in making that declaration. Whenever there is a contest between the oppressed and the oppressor—the weapons being equal between both parties, God knows my heart must be with the oppressed and always against the oppressor. Rather than see men wearing their chains in a cowardly and servile spirit, I would rather see them breaking the head of a tyrant with other chains. Give me, as a non-resistant, Bunker Hill and Lexington and Concord, rather than the cowardice and servility of a Southern slave plantation."

Again, I ask, does this echo and reverberate in the deeps of the American consciousness? Is this not the burden of our education, of our culture, of our democratic will . . . in its best phase, not in terms of the New Calvinism of the Pentagon which directs all its destructive forces against an enemy whose inate evil consists of the fact that it is as strong as, or stronger than, we are . . . but in terms of the will of a free people who want every other people to be free, who are instinctively groping for a country which is the world and countrymen who are mankind.

Reverend King often mentions Henry David Thoreau as one of his ideological guides, but he is talking about the early Thoreau. The Thoreau of *Civil Disobedience* was a passive resister; there is no doubt of this, who let his body be confined without struggling. He then believed that his meditations followed the jailor out into the world "without let or hindrance, and they were really all that was dangerous." But this was while being locked up by gentle Sam Staples, who would not have considered changing Henry's mind about anything, and being let out the next morning after Aunt Maria put a shawl over her head and came down and paid the trifling fine.

A few years later, as an aftermath of the capture and return of the fugitive Anthony Burns to the iron house of bondage, certain abolitionists who had tried forcibly to rescue him were confined in jail in Boston. Thoreau spoke of this incarceration at the anti-slavery celebration in Framingham with corrosive indignation, saying, "I had thought the house was on fire and not the prairie, but though several of the citizens of Massachusetts are now imprisoned for attempting to rescue a slave from her own clutches, not one of the speakers at the Kansas Meeting expressed regret for it, not one ever referred to it."

There is nothing here about the slave, Anthony Burns, submitting his body to confinement in a peaceful way, being content with the free exercise of his mind. Nor is there any condemnation, but only the highest praise for those citizens of Boston, led by Theodore Parker, who attempted to rescue, by force and arms, a legally adjudged, and legally confined and remanded, fugitive slave.

Thoreau had some bitter things to say about the citizens of Massachusetts who did not resist this. He hears them saying this about their public shame: "Do what you will, O Government, with my wife and children, my mother and brother, my father and sister, I will obey your commands to the letter. It will indeed grieve me if you hurt them, if you deliver them to overseas to be hunted by hounds, or to be whipped to death; but never-the-less, I will peaceably pursue my own chosen calling on this fair earth, until, perchance, one day, when I have put on mourning clothes for them dead, I shall have persuaded you to relent. Such is the attitudes, such are the words of Massachusetts."

Then he gives his side of the dialogue: "Rather than do this, I need not say what match I would touch, what system endeavor to blow up, but as I love my life, I would side with the light and let the dark earth roll from under me, calling my mother and brother to follow."

Oddly enough, here follow the words of Martin Luther King, so *like* those of the inert souls of Massachusetts men that Thoreau was trying to regenerate. "American Negroes must come to the point where they can say to their white brothers, paraphrasing the words of Gandhi, 'We will match your capacity to inflict suffering with our capacity to endure suffering. We will meet your physical force with soul force. We will not hate you, but we cannot, in good conscience, obey your unjust laws. Do to us what you will and we will still love you. Bomb our homes and threaten our children; send your hooded perpetrators of violence into our communities and drag us out on some wayside road, beating us and leaving us half dead, and we will still love you. But we will soon wear you down by our capacity to suffer. And in winning our freedom we will so appeal to your heart and consciousness that we will win you in the process."

No, I say, an everlasting No! to this. Two hundred years of appeal by accumulative suffering to the hearts of racists is enough, enough, enough! The American Negro is not a downtrodden Hindu, a palpitating mass of ingrained and inborn submission to being put in his place, a citizen of a land so impoverished and barren that a lifetime of abject starvation is the common lot, a land where living is so hard that men want a God so they can hate him.

The American Negro is a citizen in a rich land, with a citizen's rights and duty to resist; *resist* all attempts to deprive him of its manifold blessings. Why should he be urged to go through this Hindu-izing to regain the rights he already had in 1776? He was here then, you know, and

32

he fought alongside the rest of us out of the same revolutionary morality, for the same revolutionary rights now re-emphasized in the Fourteenth Amendment; the idea that all men before the law are exactly equal, and that no man can take away these equalities except as forfeiture for a crime adjudged and confirmed by ancient and democratic due process.

The Negro always had these rights by the book; they have been taken away from him only by force and fraud, which he has always resisted, but in vain. And not passively, on his knees, but on his feet, until he went down, a victim of blood and violence. Now should he be urged to suffer another hundred years of beatings, bombings, and aggressions by nothing but "soul force" and "spirituality"? Suffer again and again until the white South gets around to "loving" him? That is a lunatic society down there; they will never stop beating until the rest of the country makes them stop. If we say the Negro is a citizen then he has a clear duty to resist tyranny and dictatorship, legally and peacefully if he can, forcibly if he must. He is the birthright possessor of inalienable rights. He cannot give them up if he wants to. He was not born to be a punching bag to test the longevity of the Southern whites' desire to beat him.

In the latter pages of this book, Robert Williams also quotes Thoreau. But this is the final Thoreau, the Thoreau who shouldered for the rest of his short life, the full burden of his affinity with John Brown's revolutionary morality, as exemplified by the action at Harpers Ferry. This is a morality completely affirmed by Justice Douglas of the United States Supreme Court.

"The Declaration of Independence is our Creed," says Justice Douglas in his piece, "The U.S. and the Revolutionary Spirit." We should not be afraid to talk revolution, to voice our approval of it, he says. We should become the active protagonist of independence of all people, he says. He defines certain areas of the human condition where active struggles for change should be supported in the name of our own revolutionary tradition. He urges us to go smack up against the darkness and pain of continuing feudalism. "There is political feudalism wherever people have no voice in their affairs. There is political feudalism where a dynasty has the trappings of a parliamentary system but manipulates it for the benefit of a ruling class. . . . Revolution in the twentieth century means rebellion against another kind of feudalism . . . economic feudalism . . . the United States should promote democratic revolutions against these conditions of economic feudalism." That's what the Judge said. Those are his very words.

And this is what Williams is saying, and fighting about . . . only he says it about *us*, and millions, especially black millions, find that it is largely true. They want to struggle peacefully and democratically against this continuing feudalism. There is, after all, a Fourteenth Amendment on the books. It says quite clearly that "All persons born or naturalized in the United States, and subject to the jurisdiction thereof, are citizens of the United States and of the States wherein they reside. No State shall make or enforce any law which shall abridge the privileges and immunities of citizens of the United States, nor shall any State deprive any person of life, liberty or property, without due process of the laws, nor deny to any person within its jurisdiction, the equal protection of the laws."

It is obvious to the feeblest intelligence that this act is broken every day; every moment in the South. Every racist law, every act of exclusion because of color is a violation of it. It is also obvious that it is revolutionary, that it has the quality of continuous revolutionary principle in it. The South knows this and has resisted it with every counter-revolutionary tactic at its disposal. The men who drew this law *made* it revolutionary. The thrust of its enforcement is constantly in head-on collision with the *de facto* political structure of the South. One or the other must go down. It is a law which symbolized at the time

34

of its passage, and will still more symbolize at the moment of its full consummation, the working together of the Negro and the white to make this a government of the people. The abolitionists set it up, the defeat of the Confederacy made it imperative. It was freely admitted that it "confers on Congress the power to invade any state to enforce the freedom of the African in war or peace."

It is the root of our national tragedy and shame that this program to nationalize the inalienable rights of our citizens, a program adopted twice by constitutional amendment, once by legislative enactment over a Presidential veto, and in 1954, confirmed in its essence by the full Supreme Court, has been ruthlessly violated by a whole section of the country without, as Whitman put it, "Its own punishment following duly after in exact proportion against the smallest chance of escape."

It was the consciousness that they were citizens and men that Williams tried to implant in his community. If the Government would not protect their rights by due process, then they must do it themselves. He simply would not recognize that he, as a Negro, was barred from any of the privileges and immunities of the whites . . . particularly if those privileges were part and parcel of a governmental structure, paid for by Government funds. This conferred upon him, so he thought, a legality which superseded the racist legality of Southern municipal law. It made a virtue, an act of patriotism and faith, out of resistance.

What he did is told in the following pages . . . it was by acting out, by being a personal example of, by extolling, by poeticizing, by putting his life on the line for the day-by-day regeneration of the resistant spirit. He is not up to the Sermon on the Mount, but he has made it to Lexington Green.

If there is a real resistance movement anywhere in the Negro community, it was, and perhaps still may be, in Monroe, North Carolina. Sadly, if it was also a turning point in the liberation movement as a whole, it is not

35

enough known by the masses, by the millions, to transform them. That it should be known, that the people of the United States should have the chance to transform themselves, to drive the slave and the racist out of their deepest consciousness, go without saying.

Thoreau said about John Brown, the hardiest phophetical element the American people ever had to swallow, "Our thoughts could not revert to any great or wiser or better man with whom to contrast him, for he, then and there, was above them all. The man this country was about to hang appeared the greatest and the best in it. Years are not required for a revolution of public opinion; days, nay hours, produced marked changes in this case."

But John Brown was fully written of, was widely examined in the noonday glare of an aroused press. Williams and the brave Negro people of Monroe are either lied about, or must carry on their resistance in silence, in obscurity, in poverty and attrition; the rest of the world hardly knows what they are doing, does not even know their names. It was a little band of extremists, working quietly for many years, then brought into a state of dazzling clarity and climax by John Brown, that made viable the concepts that appear in the Fourteenth Amendment, that continuity-keeper and regenerator of our revolutionary principles. It may be that Williams and the Negroes of Monroe will finally be the means of making citizens out of all persons born or naturalized in the United States.

Robert F. Williams and his wife, Mabel, at the Plaza Ci, Habana, Cuba, March 1962 (photo by LeRoy McLucas).

WANTED BY THE FBI

INTERSTATE FLIGHT — KIDNAPING
ROBERT FRANKLIN WILLIAMS

Photograph taken May, 1961

FBI No. 84,275 B

Aliases: Bob Williams, Robert F. Williams.

DESCRIPTION

Age:	36, born February 26, 1925, Monroe, North Carolina		
Height:	6'	Complexion:	dark brown
Weight:	240 pounds	Race:	Negro
Build:	heavy	Nationality:	American
Hair:	black	Occupations:	free lance writer, freight
Eyes:	brown		handler, janitor, machinist

Scars and Marks: scar left eyelid, scar left nostril, scar on calf of right leg.

Fingerprint Classification: 19 L 1 R 100 8 Ref: T R T

M 1 T 10   A A T

CAUTION

WILLIAMS ALLEGEDLY HAS POSSESSED A LARGE QUANTITY OF FIREARMS, INCLUDING A .45 CALIBER PISTOL WHICH HE CARRIES IN HIS CAR. HE HAS PREVIOUSLY BEEN DIAGNOSED AS SCHIZOPHRENIC AND HAS ADVOCATED AND THREATENED VIOLENCE. WILLIAMS SHOULD BE CONSIDERED ARMED AND EXTREMELY DANGEROUS.

A Federal warrant was issued on August 28, 1961, at Charlotte, North Carolina, charging Williams with unlawful interstate flight to avoid prosecution for kidnaping (Title 18, U. S. Code, Section 1073).

IF YOU HAVE INFORMATION CONCERNING THIS PERSON, PLEASE NOTIFY ME OR CONTACT YOUR LOCAL FBI OFFICE. TELEPHONE NUMBER IS LISTED BELOW.

DIRECTOR
FEDERAL BUREAU OF INVESTIGATION
UNITED STATES DEPARTMENT OF JUSTICE
WASHINGTON 25, D. C.
TELEPHONE, NATIONAL 8-7117

Wanted Flyer No. 290
September 6, 1961

PROLOGUE

Why do I speak to you from exile?

Because a Negro community in the South took up guns in self-defense against racist violence—and used them. I am held responsible for this action, that for the first time in history American Negroes have armed themselves as a group, to defend their homes, their wives, their children, in a situation where law and order had broken down, where the authorities could not, or rather would not, enforce their duty to protect Americans from a lawless mob. I accept this responsibility and am proud of it. I have asserted the right of Negroes to meet the violence of the Ku Klux Klan by armed self-defense—and have acted on it. It has always been an accepted right of Americans, as the history of our Western states proves, that where the law is unable, or unwilling, to enforce order, the citizens can, and must, act in self-defense against lawless violence. I believe this right holds for black Americans as well as whites.

Many people will remember that in the summer of 1957 the Ku Klux Klan made an armed raid on an Indian community in the South and were met with determined rifle fire from the Indians acting in self-defense. The nation approved of the action and there were widespread expressions of pleasure at the defeat of the Kluxers, who showed their courage by running away despite their armed superiority. What the nation doesn't know, because it has never been told, is that the Negro community in Monroe, North Carolina, had set the example two weeks before when we shot up an armed motorcade of the Ku Klux Klan, including two police cars, which had come to attack the home of Dr. Albert E. Perry, vice-president of the Monroe chapter of the National Association for the Advancement of Colored People. The stand taken by our chapter

39

resulted in the official re-affirmation by the NAACP of the right of self-defense. The Preamble to the resolution of the 50th Convention of the NAACP, New York City, July 1959, states: ". . . we do not deny, but reaffirm, the right of an individual and collective self-defense against unlawful assaults."

Because there has been much distortion of my position, I wish to make it clear that I do not advocate violence for its own sake, or for the sake of reprisals against whites. Nor am I against the passive resistance advocated by the Reverend Martin Luther King and others. My only difference with Dr. King is that I believe in flexibility in the freedom struggle. This means that I believe in non-violent tactics where feasible and the mere fact that I have a Sit-In case pending before the U.S. Supreme Court bears this out. Massive civil disobedience is a powerful weapon under civilized conditions, where the law safeguards the citizens' right of peaceful demonstrations. In civilized society the law serves as a deterrent against lawless forces that would destroy the democratic process. But where there is a breakdown of the law, the individual citizen has a right to protect his person, his family, his home and his property. To me this is so simple and proper that it is self-evident.

When an oppressed people show a willingness to defend themselves, the enemy, who is a moral weakling and coward is more willing to grant concessions and work for a respectable compromise. Psychologically, moreover, racists consider themselves superior beings and they are not willing to exchange their superior lives for our inferior ones. They are most vicious and violent when they can practice violence with impunity. This we have shown in Monroe. Moreover, when because of our self-defense there is a danger that the blood of whites may be spilled, the local authorities in the South suddenly enforce law and order when previously they had been complaisant toward lawless, racist violence. This too we have proven in Monroe.

40

It is remarkable how easily and quickly state and local police control and disperse lawless mobs when the Negro is ready to defend himself with arms.

Furthermore, because of the international situation, the Federal Government does not want racial incidents which draw the attention of the world to the situation in the South. Negro self-defense draws such attention, and the Federal Government will be more willing to enforce law and order if the local authorities don't. When our people become fighters, our leaders will be able to sit at the conference table as equals, not dependent on the whim and the generosity of the oppressors. It will be to the best interests of both sides to negotiate just, honorable and lasting settlements.

The majority of white people in the United States have literally no idea of the violence with which Negroes in the South are treated daily—nay, hourly. This violence is deliberate, conscious, condoned by the authorities. It has gone on for centuries and is going on today, every day, unceasing and unremitting. It is our way of life. Negro existence in the South has been one long travail, steeped in terror and blood—our blood. The incidents which took place in Monroe, which I witnessed and which I suffered, will give some idea of the conditions in the South, such conditions that can no longer be borne. That is why, one hundred years after the Civil War began, we Negroes in Monroe armed ourselves in self-defense and used our weapons. We showed that our policy worked. The lawful authorities of Monroe and North Carolina acted to enforce order only after, and as a direct result of, our being armed. Previously they had connived with the Ku Klux Klan in the racist violence against our people. Self-defense prevented bloodshed and forced the law to establish order. This is the meaning of Monroe and I believe it marks a historic change in the life of my people. This is the story of that change.

Chapter 1

SELF-DEFENSE PREVENTS BLOODSHED

In June of 1961 the NAACP Chapter of Monroe, North Carolina, decided to picket the town's swimming pool. This pool, built by WPA money, was forbidden to Negroes although we formed one third the population of the town. In 1957 we had asked not for integration but for the use of the pool one day a week. This was denied and for four years we were put off with vague suggestions that someday another pool would be built. Two small Negro children had meantime drowned swimming in creeks. Now, in 1961, the City of Monroe announced it had surplus funds, but there was no indication of a pool, no indication of even an intention to have a pool. So we decided to start a picket line. We started the picket line and the picket line closed the pool. When the pool closed the racists decided to handle the matter in traditional Southern style. They turned to violence, unlawful violence.

We had been picketing for two days when we started taking lunch breaks in a picnic area reserved for "White People Only." Across from the picnic area, on the other side of a stream of water, a group of white people started firing rifles and we could hear the bullets strike the trees over our heads. The chief of police was on duty at the pool and I appealed to him to stop the firing into the picnic area. The chief of police said, "Oh, I don't hear anything. I don't hear anything at all." They continued shooting all that day. The following day these people drifted toward the picket line firing their pistols and we kept appealing to the chief of police to stop them from shooting near us. He would always say, "Well, I don't hear anything."

The pool remained closed but we continued the line and crowds of many hundreds would come to watch us and

42

shout insults at the pickets. The possibility of violence was increasing to such a proportion that we had sent a telegram to the U.S. Justice Department asking them to protect our right to picket. The Justice Department referred us to the local FBI. We called the local FBI in Charlotte and they said this was not a matter for the U.S. Justice Department; it was a local matter and that they had checked with our local chief of police, who had assured them that he would give us ample protection. This was the same chief of police who had stood idly by while these people were firing pistols and rifles over our heads. This was the same chief of police who in 1957 had placed two police cars in a Klan motorcade that raided the Negro community.

Attempt to Kill Me

On Friday, June 23, 1961, I went into town to make another telephone call to the Justice Department and while I was there I picked up one of the pickets and started back to the line at the swimming pool, which was on the outskirts of town. I was driving down U.S. Highway 74 going east when a heavy car (I was driving a small English car, a Hillman), a 1955 DeSoto sedan, came up from behind and tried to force my lighter car off the embankment and over a cliff with a 75-foot drop. I outmaneuvered him by speeding up and getting in front of him. Then he rammed my car from the rear and locked the bumper and he started a zig-zag motion across the highway in an attempt to flip my light car over. The bumpers were stuck and I didn't use the brake because I didn't want it to neutralize the front wheels.

We had to pass right by a highway patrol station. The station was in a 35-mile-an-hour zone and by the time we passed it the other car was pushing me at 70 miles an hour. I started blowing my horn incessantly, hoping to attract the attention of the highway patrolmen. There were three patrolmen standing on the opposite side of the embankment in the yard of the station. They looked at the man who was pushing and zig-zagging me across the highway and then threw up their hands, laughed, and turned their backs to the highway.

He kept pushing me for a quarter of an hour until we came to a highway intersection carrying heavy traffic. The man was hoping to run me out into the traffic, but about 75 feet away from the highway I was finally able to rock loose from his bumper, and I made a sharp turn into the ditch.

My car was damaged. The brake drum, the wheels, and the bearings had been damaged, and all of the trunk compartment in the rear had been banged in. After we got it out of the ditch, I took the car back to the swimming pool and I showed it to the chief of police. He stood up and looked at the car and laughed. He said, "I don't see anything. I don't see anything at all." I said, "You were standing here when I left." He said, "Well, I still don't see anything." So I told him I wanted a warrant for the man, whom I had recognized. He was Bynum Griffin, the Pontiac-Chevrolet dealer in Monroe. And he said, "I can't give you a warrant because I can't see anything that he's done." But a newspaperman standing there started to examine my car and when the chief of police discovered that a newspaperman was interested, then he said, "Well, come to the police station and I'll give you a warrant."

When I went to the police station he said, "Well, you just got a name and a license number and I can't indict a man on that. You can take it up with the Court Solicitor." I went to the Court Solicitor, which is equivalent to the District Attorney, and he said, "Well, all you got here is a name and a number on a piece of paper. I can't indict a man on these grounds." I told him that I recognized the man and I mentioned his name. He said, "Wait a minute," and he made a telephone call. He said, "I called him and he said he didn't do that." I again told him that I had recognized the man and that I had the license number of the car that he had used. Finally the Court Solicitor said, "Well, if you insist, I'll tell you what you do. You go to his house and take a look at him and if you recognize him, you bring him up here and I'll make out a warrant for him." I told him that was what the police were being paid for; that they were supposed to go and pick up criminals. So they refused to give me a warrant for this man at all.

"God Damn, The Niggers Have Got Guns!"

The picket line continued. On Sunday, on our way to the swimming pool, we had to pass through the same intersection (U.S. 74 and U.S. 601). There were about two or three thousand people lined along the highway. Two or three policemen were standing at the intersection directing traffic and there were two policemen who had been following us from my home. An old stock car without windows was parked by a restaurant at the intersection. As soon as we drew near, this car started backing out as fast as possible. The driver hoped to hit us in the side and flip us over. But I turned my wheel sharply and the junk car struck the front of my car and both cars went into a ditch.

Then the crowd started screaming. They said that a nigger had hit a white man. They were referring to me. They were screaming, "Kill the niggers! Kill the niggers! Pour gasoline on the niggers! Burn the niggers!"

We were still sitting in the car. The man who was driving the stock car got out of the car with a baseball bat and started walking toward us and he was saying, "Nigger, what did you hit me for?" I didn't say anything to him. We just sat there looking at him. He came up close to our car, within arm's length with the baseball bat, but I still hadn't said anything and we didn't move in the car. What they didn't know was that we were armed. Under North Carolina state law it is legal to carry firearms in your automobile so long as these firearms are not concealed.

I had two pistols and a rifle in the car. When this fellow

45

started to draw back his baseball bat, I put an Army .45 up in the window of the car and pointed it right into his face and I didn't say a word. He looked at the pistol and he didn't say anything. He started backing away from the car.

Somebody in the crowd fired a pistol and the people again started to scream hysterically, "Kill the niggers! Kill the niggers! Pour gasoline on the niggers!" The mob started to throw stones on top of my car. So I opened the door of the car and I put one foot on the ground and stood up in the door holding an Italian carbine.

All this time three policemen had been standing about fifty feet away from us while we kept waiting in the car for them to come and rescue us. Then when they saw that we were armed and the mob couldn't take us, two of the policemen started running. One ran straight to me and he grabbed me on the shoulder and said, "Surrender your weapon! Surrender your weapon!" I struck him in the face and knocked him back away from the car and put my carbine in his face and I told him we were not going to surrender to a mob. I told him that we didn't intend to be lynched. The other policeman who had run around the side of the car started to draw his revolver out of the holster. He was hoping to shoot me in the back. They didn't know that we had more than one gun. One of the students (who was seventeen years old) put a .45 in the policeman's face and told him that if he pulled out his pistol he would kill him. The policeman started putting his gun back into the holster and backing away from the car, and he fell into the ditch.

There was a very old man, an old white man out in the crowd, and he started screaming and crying like a baby and he kept crying, and he said, "God damn, God damn, what is this God damn country coming to that the niggers have got guns, the niggers are armed and the police can't even arrest them!" He kept crying and somebody led him away through the crowd.

46

Steve Pressman, who is a member of the Monroe City Council, came along and he told the chief of police to open the highway and get us out of there. The chief of police told the City Councilman, "But they've got guns!" Pressman said, "That's OK. Open the highway up and get them out of here!" They opened the highway and the man from the City Council led us through. All along the highway for almost a third of a mile people were lined on both sides of the road. And they were screaming "Kill the niggers! Kill the niggers! We aren't having any integration here! We're not going to swim with niggers!"

By the time we got to the pool, the other students who had gone on had already started the picket line. There were three or four thousand white people milling around the pool. All the city officials were there including the Mayor of Monroe. They had dark glasses on and they were standing in the crowd. And the crowd kept screaming. Then the chief of police came up to me and he said, "Surrender your gun." And I told him that I was not going to surrender any gun. That those guns were legal and that was a mob, and if he wanted those guns he could come to my house and get them after I got away from there. And then he said, "Well, if you hurt any of these white people here, God damn it, I'm going to kill you!" I don't know what made him think that I was going to let him live long enough to shoot me. He kept saying, "Surrender the gun!" while the white people kept screaming.

The City Councilman reappeared and said that the tension was bad and that there was a chance that somebody would be hurt. He conceded that I had a right to picket and he said that if I were willing to go home he would see that I was escorted. I asked him who was going to escort us home. He said "the police." I told him that I might as well go with the Ku Klux Klan as go with them. I said I would go with the police department under one condition.

He asked what that was. I told him I would take one of the students out of my car and let them put a policeman in there and then I could rest assured that they would protect us. And the police said they couldn't do that. They couldn't do that because they realized that this policeman would get hurt if they joined in with the mob.

The officials kept repeating how the crowd was getting out of hand; somebody would get hurt. I told them that I wasn't going to leave until they cleared the highway. I also told them that if necessary we would make our stand right there. Finally they asked me what did I suggest they do, and I recommended they contact the state police. So they contacted the state police and an old corporal and a young man came; just two state patrolmen. Three or four thousand people were out there, and the city had twenty-one policemen present who claimed they couldn't keep order.

The old man started cursing and told the people to move back, to spread out and to move out of there. And he started swinging a stick. Some of the mob started cursing and he said, "God damn it, I mean it. Move out." They got the message and suddenly the crowd was broken up and dispersed. The officials and state police knew that if they allowed the mob to attack us a lot of people were going to be killed, and some of those people would be white.

Two police cars escorted us out; one in front and one behind. This was the first time this had ever been done. And some of the white people started screaming "Look how they are protecting niggers! Look how they are taking niggers out of here!"

As a result of our stand, and our willingness to fight, the state of North Carolina had enforced law and order. Just two state troopers did the job, and no one got hurt in a situation where normally (in the South) a lot of Negro blood would have flowed. The city closed the pool for the rest of the year and we withdrew our picket line.

This was not the end of the story of our struggle in Monroe in 1961. By a quirk of fate the next episode involved the Freedom Riders and their policy of passive resistance. The contrast between the results of their policy and the results of our policy of self-defense is a dramatic object lesson for all Negroes. But before I go on to that I have to describe how our policy of self-defense developed and how the Negro community in Monroe came to support my conclusion that we had to "meet violence with violence."

The story begins in 1955 when, as a veteran of the U.S. Marine Corps, I returned to my home town of Monroe and joined the local chapter of the NAACP.

Chapter 2

AN NAACP CHAPTER
IS REBORN IN MILITANCY

My home town is Monroe, North Carolina. It has a population of 11,000, about a third of which is Negro. It is a county seat (Union County) and is 14 miles from the South Carolina border. Its spirit is closer to that of South Carolina than to the liberal atmosphere of Chapel Hill which people tend to associate with North Carolina. There are no trade unions in our county and the south-eastern regional headquarters of the Ku Klux Klan is in Monroe.

There was also, at the time of my return, a small and dwindling chapter of the NAACP. The Union County NAACP was a typical Southern branch—small, not very active, dominated by, and largely composed of, the upper crust of the black community—professionals, businessmen and white-collar workers.

Before the Supreme Court desegregation decision of 1954, the NAACP was not a primary target of segregationists. In many places in the South, including Monroe, racists were not too concerned with the small local chapters. But the Supreme Court decision drastically altered this casual attitude. The Ku Klux Klan and the White Citizens Councils made it their business to locate any NAACP chapter in their vicinity, and to find out who its officers and members were. Threats of violence and economic sanctions were applied to make people withdraw their membership. Chapters, already small, dwindled rapidly.

A Veteran Returns Home

When I got out of the Marine Corps, I knew I wanted to go home and join the NAACP. In the Marines I had

50

got a taste of discrimination and had some run-ins that got me into the guardhouse. When I joined the local chapter of the NAACP it was going down in membership, and when it was down to six, the leadership proposed dissolving it. When I objected, I was elected president and they withdrew, except for Dr. Albert E. Perry. Dr. Perry was a newcomer who had settled in Monroe and built up a very successful practice, and he became our vice-president. I tried to get former members back without success and finally I realized that I would have to work without the social leaders of the community.

At this time I was inexperienced. Before going into the Marines I had left Monroe for a time and worked in an aircraft factory in New Jersey and an auto factory in Detroit. Without knowing it, I had picked up some ideas of organizing from the activities around me, but I had never served in a union local and I lacked organizing experience. But I am an active person and I hated to give up on something so important as the NAACP.

So one day I walked into a Negro poolroom in our town, interrupted a game by putting NAACP literature on the table and made a pitch. I recruited half of those present. This got our chapter off to a new start. We began a recruiting drive among laborers, farmers, domestic workers, the unemployed and any and all Negro people in the area. We ended up with a chapter that was unique in the whole NAACP because of working class composition and a leadership that was not middle class. Most important, we had a strong representation of returned veterans who were very militant and who didn't scare easy. We started a struggle in Monroe and Union County to integrate public facilities and we had the support of a Unitarian group of white people. In 1957, without any friction at all, we integrated the public library. It shocked us that in other Southern states, particularly Virginia, Negroes encountered such violence in trying to integrate libraries.

We moved on to win better rights for Negroes: economic

rights, the right of education and the right of equal protection under the law. We rapidly got the reputation of being the most militant branch of the NAACP, and obviously we couldn't get this reputation without antagonizing the racists who are trying to prevent Afro-Americans from enjoying their inalienable human rights as Americans. Specifically, we aroused the wrath of the Ku Klux Klan and a showdown developed over the integration of the swimming pool.

The Ku Klux Klan Swings into Action

As I said, the swimming pool had been built with Federal funds under the WPA system and was supported by municipal taxation; yet Negroes could not use this pool. Neither the Federal government nor the local officials had provided any swimming facilities at all for Negroes. Over a period of years several of our children had drowned while swimming in unsupervised swimming holes. When we lost another child in 1956 we started a drive to obtain swimming facilities for Negroes, especially for our children.

First, we asked the city officials to build a pool in the Negro community. This would have been a segregated pool, but we asked for this because we were merely interested in safe facilities for the children. The city officials said they couldn't comply with this request, for it would be too expensive and they didn't have the money. Then, in a compromise move, we asked that they set aside one or two days out of each week when the segregated pool would be reserved for Negro children. When we asked for this they said that this too would be too expensive. Why would it be too expensive, we asked. Because, they said, each time the colored people used the pool they would have to drain the water and refill it.

They said they would eventually build us a pool when they got the funds. We asked them when we could expect it. One year? They said No. We asked, five years? They said No, they couldn't be sure. We asked, ten years? They said that they couldn't be sure. We asked finally if we could expect it within fifteen years and they said that they couldn't give us any definite promise.

There was a white Catholic priest in the community who owned a station wagon and he would transport the colored youth to Charlotte, N.C., which was twenty-five miles away, so they could swim there in the Negro pool. Some of the city officials of Charlotte saw this priest swimming in the Negro pool and they wanted to know who he was. The Negro supervisor explained that he was a priest. The city officials replied they didn't care whether he was a priest or not, that he was white and they had segregation of the races in Charlotte; so they barred the priest from the colored pool.

Again the children didn't have any safe place to swim at all—so we decided to take legal action against the Monroe pool.

First, we started a campaign of stand-ins of short duration. We would go stand for a few minutes and ask to be admitted and never get admitted. While we were preparing the groundwork for possible court proceedings, the Ku Klux Klan came out in the open. The press started to carry articles about the Klan activities. In the beginning they mentioned that a few hundred people would gather in open fields and have their Klan rallies. Then the numbers kept going up. The numbers went up to 3,000, 4,000, 5,000. Finally the *Monroe Inquirer* estimated that 7,500 Klansmen had gathered in a field to discuss dealing with the integrationists, described by the Klan as the "Communist-Inspired-National-Association-for-the-Advancement-of-Colored-People." They started a campaign to get rid of us, to drive us out of the community, directed primarily at Dr. Albert E. Perry, our vice-president, and at myself.

The Klan started by circulating a petition. To gather signatures they set up a table in the county courthouse square in Monroe. The petition stated that Dr. Perry and I should be permanently driven out of Union County because we were members and officials of the Communist-NAACP. The Klan claimed 3,000 signatures in the first week. In the following week they claimed 3,000 more. They had no basis for any legal action, but they had hoped to frighten us out of town just by virtue of sheer numbers. In the history of the South, in days past, it was enough to know that so many people wanted to get rid of a Negro to make him take off by himself. One must remember that in this community where the press estimated that there were 7,500 Klan supporters, the population of the town was only about 12,000 people. Actually, many of the Klan people came in from South Carolina, Monroe being only fourteen miles from the state border.

When they discovered that this could not intimidate us, they decided to take direct action. After their rallies they would drive through our community in motorcades and they would honk their horns and fire pistols from the car windows. On one occasion, they caught a colored woman on an isolated street corner and they made her dance at pistol point.

At this outbreak of violence against our Negro community, a group of pacifist ministers went to the city officials and asked that the Klan be prohibited from forming these motorcades to parade through Monroe. The officials of the county and the city rejected their request on the grounds that the Klan was a legal organization having as much constitutional right to organize as the NAACP.

Self-Defense Is Born of Our Plight

Since the city officials wouldn't stop the Klan, we decided to stop the Klan ourselves. We started this action out of the need for defense, because law and order had completely vanished; because there was no such thing as a 14th Amendment to the United States Constitution in Monroe, N.C. The local officials refused to enforce law and order and when we turned to Federal and state officials

54

Above: Arms in the Perry living room. Dr. Perry at left, next is Robert F. Williams.

Below: Guards at Dr. Perry's home with odd assembly of weapons.

CAROLINA
EDITION

Journal and Guide

VOL LVII No. 41   NORFOLK, VIRGINIA, SATURDAY, OCTOBER 12, 1957   20 PAGES   PRICE 15 CENTS

ASIAN FLU...
"What To Do
Helpful Advice from an Expert
Page 20

CITIZENS FIRE BACK AT KLAN

One of the few papers that covered the attack of the Ku Klux Klan on Dr. Perry's home and the shooting back by defenders. The national press remained silent.

Ku Kluxers Use Guns At Monroe, NC

Shots Exchanged Near Residence Of NAACP Head

Special to Journal and Guide

MONROE, N. C. — It has been reported here that a group of Ku Klux Klansmen, some of them robed and masked, swapped gunfire with a group of colored citizens near the home of the president of the local NAACP branch late Friday night.

Police officials say that no shots were fired, but Union county NAACP Vice - President Robert F. Williams said

fired on a group of some 30 to 40 colored citizens near the home of the NAACP president, Dr. A. F. Perry.

* * *

MR. WILLIAMS also said that when someone in the colored gathering returned the fire, police officers came over to disarm them.

Police Chief A. A. Mauney has a different version of the affair. He says that several police cars were at the caravan of "about 30 cars" that "disbanded" when a train cut across its path. The chief said that he instructed his men to get in front of the caravan and if any violations occurred to stop the procession.

* * *

EVEN TOUGH North Carolina law forbids the wearing of masks by adults in public gathering, Chief Mauney said that he had had no reports that some of the Klansmen were masked.

Police officers in cars in the area said that they did hear "what sounded like a shot from near the doctor's house" even though they deny

to enforce law and order they either refused or ignored our appeals.

Luther Hodges, who is now Secretary of Commerce, was the Governor of North Carolina at that time. We first appealed to him. He took sides with the Klan; they had not broken any laws, they were not disorderly. Then we appealed to President Eisenhower but we never received a reply to our telegrams. There was no response at all from Washington.

So we started arming ourselves. I wrote to the National Rifle Association in Washington which encourages veterans to keep in shape to defend their native land, and asked for a charter, which we got. In a year we had sixty members. We had bought some guns too, in stores, and later a church in the North raised money and got us better rifles. The Klan discovered we were arming and guarding our community. In the summer of 1957 they made one big attempt to stop us. An armed motorcade attacked Dr. Perry's house, which is situated on the outskirts of the colored community. We shot it out with the Klan and repelled their attack and the Klan didn't have any more stomach for this type of fight. They stopped raiding our community. After this clash the same city officials who said the Klan had a constitutional right to organize met in an emergency session and passed a city ordinance banning the Klan from Monroe without a special permit from the police chief.

At the time of our clash with the Klan only three Negro publications—the *Afro-American*, the *Norfolk Journal and Guide*, and *Jet Magazine*—reported the fight. *Jet* carried some pictures of the self-defense guard. Our fight occurred two weeks before the famous clash between the Indians and the Klan. We had driven the Klan out of our county into the Indian territory. The national press played up the Indian-Klan fight because they didn't consider this a great threat—the Indians are a tiny minority and people could laugh at the incident as a sentimental joke—but no one wanted Negroes to get the impression that this was an accepted way to deal with the Klan. So the white press maintained a complete blackout about the Monroe fight.

After the Klan learned that violence wouldn't serve their purpose they started to use the racist courts. Dr. Perry, our vice-president, was indicted on a trumped-up charge of abortion. He is a Catholic physician, and one of the doctors who had been head of the county medical department drove forty miles to testify in Dr. Perry's behalf, declaring that when Dr. Perry had worked in the hospital he had refused to file sterilization permits for the County Welfare Department on the ground that this was contrary to his religious beliefs. But he was convicted, sentenced to five years in prison, and the loss of his medical license.

* * *

The Kissing Case

In October, 1958, two local colored boys, David Simpson, aged 7, and Hanover Thompson, aged 9, were arrested on the charge of rape, which is punishable in North Carolina by death.

This was the famous "Kissing Case." What had happened was that David and Hanover got into a game of "cowboys and Indians" with some white children one afternoon. After a while, the white girls in the group suggested they play "house." One of the little white girls, Sissy Marcus, sat on Hanover's lap and suddenly recognized Hanover as her old playmate. For Hanover's mother worked for Sissy's mother and until Hanover reached school age his mother had taken him with her when she went to work at the Marcus house.

When this little girl discovered that Hanover was her old playmate she kissed him on the cheek. Later on in the afternoon she ran home and told her mother how she had seen Hanover and how she was so happy to see him again that she had kissed him.

58

Mrs. Marcus got hysterical when she heard this and she called the police. Before the two boys had even gotten home they were arrested and thrown into the county jail. If a person is arrested for rape in North Carolina he is not permitted to see anyone for a period of time while the police investigate. Therefore the police didn't notify the boys' parents.

A few days later when we finally found out what had happened and where the two missing boys were, we tried to get help. But the national office of the NAACP wouldn't have anything to do with the case because it was a "sex case." A seven-year-old white girl had kissed a nine-year-old Negro boy on the cheek and the national office didn't want any part of it.

The children were sent to the reformatory soon after they were arrested. I called the civil rights lawyer, Conrad Lynn, and he came down from New York. First thing, he went to talk with Judge Hampton Price, who had passed sentence.

The Judge said to Lynn that he had held a "separate but equal hearing." Lynn asked him what he meant by a "separate but equal hearing." And the Judge told him how on the morning of the trial he had called in Mrs. Marcus and her daughter, and Mrs. Marcus had made a statement, and they were sent home, and then in the afternoon the two Negro mothers were summoned to the Judge, and their boys were brought in. Then the Judge said to Lynn, "I told them what Mrs. Marcus had told me and then since they were guilty—I sent them up for fourteen years at the reformatory."

The NAACP national office still wasn't doing anything about the case but an English reporter who was a friend of Lynn's visited the reformatory and sneaked out a photograph of the boys, which appeared along with a story on the front page of the Dec. 15, 1958, *London Observer*. Then all of Europe got wind of the case and there were protest demonstrations in London, Rotterdam, Rome, and

Paris. And only then did many American newspapers begin to express "concern" about the "Kissing Case."

At the end of December, 1958, Dr. Perry, Conrad Lynn, and I were called to New York by Roy Wilkins and he offered me a job in Detroit if I'd leave Monroe. I flatly refused his offer.

By now so much pressure was building up abroad and even in the U.S.A. that the NAACP national office entered the case—this case that had until now involved such dreadful sexual implications. In late January there was a hearing, but the children were sent back to the reformatory. Meanwhile, world pressure was mounting. An example is that of the petition signed by the 15,000 students and faculty at a Rotterdam, Holland, high school named after Franklin Delano Roosevelt. The petition called for the release of the children and it was sent to Mrs. Roosevelt.

Somebody said something, finally, to President Eisenhower, and finally he said something to our then Governor Hodges and on Feb. 13, 1959, the children were released.

* * *

"We Will Meet Violence With Violence"

In 1959 Mrs. Georgia White, a Negro mother of five children, who worked in a Monroe hotel as a maid, was kicked down a flight of stairs into the lobby of the hotel by a white guest. He said he kicked Mrs. White down a flight of stairs because she had been making too much noise while working in the corridor, and had disturbed his sleep. When we asked for an indictment, the chief of police, A. A. Mauney, refused our request. Finally when we threatened to take legal action by bringing in NAACP lawyers he relented and placed this man under a $75 bond. Even though this white defendant subsequently failed to appear in court for his trial, he was not indicted.

That same day there was another colored woman in

From French press. Caption on photo says "Imprisoned for a kiss!"

LA GAUCHE

ORGANE DE COMBAT SOCIALISTE

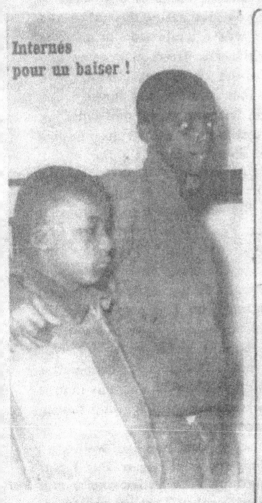

**Internés
pour un baiser !**

Voir l'article d'Ernest Glinne
en page 5

QUI SEME
LE VENT...

L E climat social se détériore rapidement. La réaction multiplie ses coups d'épingles contre le mouvement syndical. Cela irrite les travailleurs. Mais aux coups d'épingles succèdent des attaques contre leur niveau de vie. Et ces attaques ne provoquent pas seulement l'irritation mais la colère.

La Gauche

court, Mrs. Mary Ruth Reed. Mrs. Reed was eight months pregnant. She was the victim of an attempted rape by a white man who came to her house, drove her from her house, and then beat her. He caught her while she was trying to escape down the main highway and he knocked her to the ground. Mrs. Reed's six-year-old boy was running along on the side and when the white rapist beat his mother the boy picked up a stick and started hitting the man over the head with it while his mother escaped. She went to a neighbor's house and her neighbor called the police and gave her aid. The neighbor was a white woman and she came to court that day with Mrs. Reed. She came and testified that she had seen the defendant chasing Mrs. Reed and that Mrs. Reed had come to her house in an excited and hysterical state, without shoes, and with her clothes torn from her. This testimony required considerable courage on the part of Mrs. Reed's white neighbor.

During the trial the defense attorney arranged for the defendant's wife to sit at his side just as if she were also involved in the case. Then the defense attorney appealed to the jury. He said, "Judge, Your Honor, and ladies and gentlemen of the jury, you see this man. This is his wife. This woman, this white woman is the pure flower of life. She is one of God's lovely creatures, a pure flower. And do you think this man would have left this pure flower for that?" And he made it appear as if the colored woman was actually on trial. Then the defense ended by saying, "It's just a matter of whether or not you're going to believe this woman or this white man. Judge, Your Honor, this man is not guilty of any crime. He was just drinking and having a little fun." The man was acquitted.

Mrs. Reed had several brothers, and they had wanted to kill her white attacker before the trial began. But I persuaded them not to do anything. I said that this was a matter that would be handled legally. That we would get a lawyer—which we did. We brought a lawyer all the way from New York who wasn't even allowed to take the floor in court. So I was responsible for this would-be rapist not being punished.

The courtroom was full of colored women and when this man was acquitted they turned to me and they said, "Now what are you going to do? You have opened the floodgates on us. Now these people know that they can do anything that they want to us and there is no prospect of punishment under law and it means that we have been exposed to these people and you're responsible for it. Now what are you going to say?" And I told them that in a civilized society the law is a deterrent against the strong who would take advantage of the weak, but the South is not a civilized society; the South is a social jungle, so in cases like that we had to revert to the law of the jungle; that it had become necessary for us to create our own deterrent. And I said that in the future we would defend our women and children, our homes and ourselves with our arms. That we would meet violence with violence.

My statement was reprinted all over the United States. What I had said was, "This demonstration today shows that the Negro in the South cannot expect justice in the courts. He must convict his attackers on the spot. He must meet violence with violence, lynching with lynching."

The next day in an interview with the *Carolina Times* I again pointed to the lack of protection from the courts. I said, "These court decisions open the way to violence. I do not mean that Negroes should go out and attempt to get revenge for mistreatments or injustices ..." I made this statement again on the same day over a Cincinnati radio station and later that evening in a telecast interview in Charlotte I again made clear I spoke of self-defense when the courts failed to protect us.

Since the principle is so obvious, I couldn't understand the commotion my statement aroused, or why it should receive so much national publicity. Two years previously, when we had shot up the Ku Klux Klan in self-defense not a single white newspaper in America reported the incident.

63

We were only serving notice that we would do more of the same, that Negro self-defense was here to stay in Monroe. So I didn't feel we were doing anything new. I realize now that we were establishing a principle, born out of our experience, which could, and would, set an example to others.

Looking back, it is clear that racists made a big error in publicizing our stand. Even though it has caused me and my family a great deal of suffering, the result has been to force a debate on the issue and it shook up the NAACP considerably out of its timid attitudes and forced an official reaffirmation from the NAACP of the right of Negroes to self-defense against racist violence.

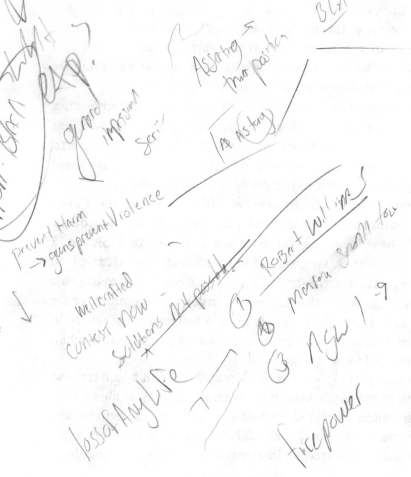

Chapter 3

THE STRUGGLE FOR
MILITANCY IN THE NAACP

Until my statement hit the national newspapers the national office of the NAACP had paid little attention to us. We had received little help from them in our struggles and our hour of need. Now they lost no time. The very next morning I received a long distance telephone call from the national office wanting to know if I had been quoted correctly. I told them that I had. They said the NAACP was not an organization of violence. I explained that I knew that it was not an organization of violence. Then they said that I had made violent statements. I replied that I made. statements as Robert Williams, not as the National Association for the Advancement of Colored People. They said that, well, because I was an official of the organization anything that I said would be considered NAACP policy. That we were too close together. And I asked them why if we were so close together they hadn't come to my rescue all this time when I had been the unemployed victim of the Klan's economic pressure and when I had had all of my insurance canceled as a poor insurance risk. I asked them why they didn't then consider our closeness.

Suspension, Distortion & Re-election

In the next few hours Roy Wilkins of the NAACP suspended me from office. I didn't learn about it from the national office. I first heard that I was suspended when Southern radio stations announced and kept repeating every thirty minutes that the NAACP had suspended me for advocating violence because this was not a means for the solution of the race problem and that the NAACP was against Negroes using violence as a means of self-defense.

65

Our Union County NAACP was one of the few interracial branches in the South. We had some white pacifist members, and when I was suspended they sent a telegram to the national office stating that they were white Southerners and that they were pacifists, but they protested my suspension on the ground that they understood the problems in the community and that the national office did not. This telegram was never made public by the NAACP. And not a single paper ever printed the fact that ours was an interracial branch and that even Southern white pacifists supported my position.

Nevertheless, this all developed into a national debate. We found out that there was no provision in the NAACP constitution to justify or authorize this hypocritical action by Roy Wilkins. I demanded some sort of hearing. Wilkins turned the matter over to the NAACP's paternalistic Committee on Branches and in New York City on June 3, 1959, they conducted what turned out to be a trial where I fought the suspension. The committee ruled that I was to be suspended for six months time, after which I would automatically be reinstated.

I didn't think of doing anything more about the suspension; there was a more important matter at hand. As a result of the trial I was more convinced than ever that one of our greatest and most immediate needs was better communication within the race. The real Afro-American struggle was merely a disjointed network of pockets of resistance and the shameful thing about it was that Negroes were relying upon the white man's inaccurate reports as their sources of information about these isolated struggles. I went home and concentrated all of my efforts into developing a newsletter that would in accurate and no uncertain terms inform both Negroes and whites of Afro-American liberation struggles taking place in the United States and about the particular struggle we were constantly fighting in Monroe. The first issue of *The Crusader* came off the mimeograph machine June 26, 1959.

Then at the last minute I decided to appeal the committee's decision to the NAACP's 50th National Convention, which was meeting in New York that July. The national office found it necessary to issue a special convention pamphlet attacking me. Their pamphlet tried to intentionally confuse my demand that Negroes meet violence with violence as a means of self-defense with the advocacy of lynch law. In its own way, the national office contributed to the erroneous impression played up by the racist press that I was agitating for race war and the indiscriminate slaughter of white people.

My suspension was upheld by the convention delegates, many of whom either felt or were pressured into seeing the vote as a question of publicly supporting or disavowing the NAACP national leadership. But on the real issue at hand, delegate sentiment forced the national leadership to support the concept of self-defense. The preamble to the resolutions passed by that convention read, ". . . we do not deny but reaffirm the right of an individual and collective self-defense against unlawful assaults."

While I was suspended, the people in my branch voted to make my wife president to serve in my place. And at the end of the six months, instead of going back into office automatically, I held an election because I didn't want the NAACP national office to think that they were doing me any special favor. We had the election and I was re-elected unanimously.

The national office of the NAACP was determined to keep within the good graces of a lot of the influential Northern whites who were disturbed by our militancy. They maintained an indifferent attitude to our branch. We had a charter and that was all. We were unable to secure assistance from them in any of our school integration cases and our sit-in cases.

In 1960 we started a sit-in campaign. We became the thirteenth town in North Carolina to start sit-in demonstrations. Though the NAACP wasn't taking notice, our sit-ins proved that self-defense and non-violence could be successfully combined. There was less violence in the Monroe sit-ins than in any other sit-ins in the South. In other communities there were Negroes who had their skulls fractured; but not a single demonstrator was even spat upon during our sit-ins. We had less violence because we'd shown the willingness and readiness to fight and defend ourselves. We didn't appear on the streets of Monroe as beggars depending upon the charity and generosity of white supremacists. We appeared as people with strength; and it was to the *mutual* advantage of all parties concerned that peaceful relations be maintained.

While the demonstrations were taking place I was arrested and finally sentenced to serve thirty days on the chain gang. The NAACP was supposed to handle my case. They handled it up to the State Supreme Court, but then they dropped my case from appeal without telling me and with only a few days left in which to file an appeal. I discovered this through the newspapers because my case had been consolidated with that of seven students from Chapel Hill, N. C. The newspapers listed the names of the defendants whose NAACP lawyers had filed appeals and I was the only one in the group whose name did not appear. I appealed to the Emergency Civil Liberties Committee. They took my case up and filed an appeal to the U.S. Supreme Court.

✳ ✳ ✳

"A Letter from De Boss"

All this did not mean that the NAACP national office was short on advice. While they did not feel responsible enough to take the appeal to higher courts, they did feel responsible enough to send me a letter upon my return from Cuba in the summer of 1960. I subsequently made two trips to Cuba.

My experiences in Monroe and with the NAACP which had resulted in launching *The Crusader* were also sharpening my awareness of the struggles of Negroes in every part of the world, how they were treated, their victories and their defeats. It was clear from the first days that Afro-Cubans were part of the Cuban revolution on a basis of complete equality and my trips confirmed this fact. A Negro, for example, was head of the Cuban armed forces and no one could hide that fact from us here in America. To me this revolution was a real thing, not one of those phony South American palace revolutions. There was a real drive to bring social justice to all the Cubans, including the black ones. Beginning late in 1959 I had begun to run factual articles about Cuba in *The Crusader,* pointing up the racial equality that existed there. The articles seem to have stirred up the national office for they sent me a letter which included statements such as these:

". . . I wonder, however, whether you are fully aware of the dangers and disadvantages of the course of action you seem to favor. I have followed closely the events in Cuba in recent months and in particular, Dr. Castro's visit to the United Nations this fall. Regardless of the merits of the Cuban cause I was greatly disturbed by the frequent show of insincerity which, I believe, should give you food for thought before you find yourself used as just another pawn in the present unfortunate feud between Cuba and our country.

". . . It is a callous interference in a native American problem and should be recognized as such by anyone in a responsible position of leadership in the American Negro movement.

". . . the present Cuban attempts to endear themselves to American Negroes are obviously caused by ulterior motives. (Let me just ask you how the American Negro tourist would feel in Cuba at the constant chant of 'Cuba si, Yanqui no!')

". . . Are you willing to forsake the important support of that section of the people who are equally opposed to suppression of Negro rights in our country?

69

". . . Does not the unfortunate example of the great American Negro singer Paul Robeson show you the dangers and mistakes of the road which you seem to be choosing? What has Paul Robeson with all his greatness done for the American Negro in his present struggle for equality: The answer, regrettable as it is, must be: Nothing."

These excerpts were reprinted in *The Crusader* and replied to in this way:

"Only a fool or a mercenary hypocrite could muster the gall to call a nation and its great leader insincere in dealing with the captive blacks of North America when in the course of their daily lives they display the greatest measure of racial equality and social justice in the world today. It is certainly a first magnitude truism that social justice starts at home and spreads abroad. In past months I have twice been to Cuba and there is nothing insincere about my being made to feel that I was a member of the human race for the first time in my life. If this is America's idea of insincerity, then heaven help this nation to become *insincere* like Fidel Castro and Free Cuba in granting persons of African descent entrance into the human race.

"As for my being 'used as a pawn in the struggle of Cuba' against imperialist and racist North America, I prefer to be on the side of right than on the side of Jim Crow and oppression. I prefer to be used as an instrument to convey the truth of a people who respect the rights of man, rather than to be used as an Uncle Tom whitewasher of black oppression and injustice and an apologist for America's hypocrisy. Cuba's aversion for America's inhumanity to man is not an interference in a 'native American problem.' It is common knowledge that the master race of the 'free world' is out to export North American manufactured racism. Racism in the U.S.A. is as much a world problem as was Nazism. If the U.S.A. is to to be the only nation exempt from the Human Rights Charter of the United Nations, then that august body is a party to the great transgressions against America's captive people. I, for one, refuse to remain silent and cooperate with the very force that is seeking after my destruction.

"The racists in America are the most brutal people on earth. It is foolhardy for an oppressed Afro-American to take the attitude that we should keep this life-death struggle a family affair. We are the oppressed, it is only natural for us to air our grievances at home and abroad. This race fight in the U.S.A. is no more a fight to be fought just by Americans than is the fight for black liberation to be conducted by colored only. Any struggle for freedom in the world today affects the stability of the whole society of man. Why would you make our struggle an exception?

"I am not afraid of alienating white friends of our liberation movement. If they really believe in freedom they will not resent deviation from the old worn path that has led us in fruitless circles. If they are insincere they are no more than Trojan horses infiltrating our ranks to strike us a treacherous, nefarious blow on behalf of those and that which they pretend to detest. For if they resent our becoming truly liberated, they will detest us for not following their misguidance and skillful subterfuge designed to prevent our arrival to the promised land. They speak much of tolerance, but they display unlimited intolerance toward those Afro-Americans who refuse to become their puppets and yes-man Uncle Toms.

"It is strange that I am asked how a 'Negro' American tourist would feel in Cuba hearing the constant chant of 'Cuba Si, Yanqui No!' No one has bothered to ask how it feels to constantly face 'White Only' signs. These signs mean "White yes, Colored no!' No one has asked me how it feels to be marched under guard with felons along a public street to jail for sitting on a 'white only' stool. On hearing 'Cuba Si, Yanqui No!' and having lived all of my life under American oppression, I was emotionally moved to join the liberation chorus. I knew it didn't apply to me because the white Christians of the 'free world' have excluded me from everything 'yanqui.'

"You make a cardinal mistake when you fail to give the great Paul Robeson credit for making a great contribution to the American 'Negro' struggle. Paul Robeson is living proof that the Afro-American need not look upon the United States as 'Nigger heaven' and the last stop for us on this earth. Paul is living proof that other civilized societies honor and respect black people for the things that 'Free America' curses, oppresses and starves for. Paul has proven that all black men are not for sale for thirty pieces of silver. He has lit a candle that many of the new generation will follow.

"Yes, wherever there is oppression in the world today, it is the concern of the entire race. My cause is the same as the Asians against the imperialist. It is the same as the African against the white savage. It is the same as Cuba against the white supremacist imperialist. When I become a part of the mainstream of American life, based on universal justice, then and then only can I see a possible mutual cause for unity against outside interference."

*　　*　　*

I don't want to leave the impression that I am against the NAACP; on the contrary I think it's an important weapon in the freedom struggle and I want to strengthen it. I don't think they should be worrying about Cuba when there is plenty to worry about in our country. They know, as I know, the extent to which the state governments and the Federal government ignored our appeals for help and for protection.

Hypocrisy and Run-around

After we closed the pool, as I've already described, the racists in Monroe went wild. On that same day, after we had gone home, a mob dragged a colored man from his car and took him out into the woods where they beat him and stood him up against a tree and threatened to shoot him. I had called the Associated Press and the UPI and reported that this man had been kidnapped and I also called the Justice Department. Apparently just when this man's attackers were getting ready to shoot him the chief of police came out and rescued him. How did the chief of police know where to find him in the woods? Later on this Negro was unable to indict anyone who had attacked him even though he recognized some of the members of the would-be lynch mob. The FBI refused to demand any indictments for kidnapping.

The racists would come through the colored community at night and fire guns and we had an exchange of gunfire on a number of occasions. One night an armed attack was led on my house by a sergeant of the State National Guard. He was recognized, but no action was taken against him. And the chief of police denied that an attack had taken place. We kept appealing to the Federal government. It was necessary to keep a guard of about twenty volunteers going every night—men who volunteered to sleep at my house and to walk guard. This was the only way that we could ward off attacks by the racists. The telephone would ring around the clock, sometimes every fifteen minutes, with threatening calls.

Then through my newsletter, *The Crusader*, I started appealing to readers everywhere to protest to the U.S. government, to the U.S. Justice Department; to protest the fact that the 14th Amendment did not exist in Monroe and that the city officials, the local bureau of the FBI in Charlotte, and the Governor of the state of North Carolina were in a conspiracy to deny Monroe Negroes their Constitutional rights.

One of the readers of *The Crusader* wrote to Congressman Kowalski of Connecticut, who in turn wrote a letter to the Attorney General, Robert Kennedy. He said that he had been appalled to learn about the lawlessness in Monroe, and how this was damaging to our country at a time when the United States was claiming to be a champion of democracy in the world. The Congressman asked for an investigation. But despite all those letters and telegrams to the U.S. Justice Department, no investigation was made. The only investigation they made was to ask our chief of police if these things were true. The chief of police assured them that they were not.

Finally I went to the Charlotte bureau of the FBI and filed a long report calling for a Federal indictment of the chief of police for denying citizens their rights guaranteed by the 14th Amendment. This report was filed, but I never heard from the FBI. Later a newspaperman told me that he had heard from the Justice Department and that they claimed they could find no evidence of any violation of the 14th Amendment in Monroe. They never did bother to answer me.

Yet it was at this time that I received a letter from the United States Department of State. In this letter they denied my family and me the right to travel to Cuba, where we had been invited for the 26th of July celebration. And the grounds for their refusal were: "because of the break in diplomatic relations between the United States and Cuba, the government of the United States cannot extend normal protective services to its citizens visiting Cuba."

This false pretense of being interested in protecting me was a farce of the first magnitude and classic hypocrisy. Numerous threats and four attempts of murder had been made on my life in the preceding three weeks and the would-be assassins, aided and abetted by local officials, were offered immunity from law by the deliberate silence of Federal officials to whom I had continuously appealed for "normal protective services." The Federal government couldn't possibly have been interested in protection for me and my family, for they passed up many opportunities to protect us here at home.

This all happened a month before I was forced to leave Monroe.

Chapter 4

NON-VIOLENCE EMBOLDENS
THE RACISTS: A WEEK OF TERROR

In our branch of the NAACP there was a general feel-
ing that we were in a deep and bitter struggle against
racists and that we needed to involve as many Negroes
as possible and to make the struggle as meaningful as possible. We felt that the single issue of the swimming pool
was too narrow for our needs, that what we needed was a
broad program with special attention to jobs, welfare, and
other economic needs.

I think this was an important step forward. The struggles of the Freedom Riders and the Sit-In Movements
have concentrated on a single goal: the right to eat at a
lunch counter, the right to sit anywhere on a bus. These
are important rights because their denial is a direct personal assault on a Negro's dignity. It is important for the
racists to maintain these peripheral forms of segregation.
They establish an atmosphere that supports a system. By
debasing and demoralizing the black man in small personal
matters, the system eats away the sense of dignity and
pride which are necessary to challenge a racist system.
But the fundamental core of racism is more than atmosphere—it can be measured in dollars and cents and unem-
ployment percentages. We therefore decided to present
a program that ranged from the swimming pool to jobs.

The Monroe Program

On Aug. 15, 1961, on behalf of our Chapter I presented
to the Monroe Board of Aldermen a ten point program
that read as follows:

PETITION

We, the undersigned citizens of Monroe, petition the City
Board of Aldermen to use its influence to endeavor to:

75

1. Induce factories in this county to hire without discrimination.
2. Induce the local employment agency to grant non-whites the same privileges given to whites.
3. Instruct the Welfare Agency that non-whites are entitled to the same privileges, courtesies and consideration given to whites.
4. Construct a swimming pool in the Winchester Avenue area of Monroe.
5. Remove all signs in the city of Monroe designating one area for colored and another for whites.
6. Instruct the Superintendent of Schools that he must prepare to desegregate the city schools no later than 1962.
7. Provide adequate transportation for all school children.
8. Formally request the State Medical Board to permit Dr. Albert E. Perry, Jr., to practice medicine in Monroe and Union County.
9. Employ Negroes in skilled or supervisory capacities in the City Government.
10. ACT IMMEDIATELY on all of these proposals and inform the committee and the public of your actions.

(signed)

Robert F. Williams
Albert E. Perry, Jr., M.D.
John W. McDow

Our demands for equal employment rights were the most important of the ten points. Many plants were moving in from the North—runaway industry from the North moving in to avoid labor unions and seeking low-priced workers in the South. They received considerable tax-supported concessions from the local Industrial Development Commission, and they didn't hire any Negroes. In fact, local bigoted officials had done everything in their power to prevent Negroes from obtaining employment. They had even gone so far as to stipulate that the new industries could not hire Afro-Americans if they expected the special concessions made possible through the taxation of us all. This amounted to taxation without representation; and it was one of our biggest complaints.

As a result of this racist policy, out of approximately 3,000 Afro-Americans in Monroe, there are 1,000 unemployed—persons unable to obtain jobs even as janitors, maids, or porters. And maids and porters, when employed,

76

earn at most $15 for a six-day week. One of the few kinds of work available, cotton picking, pays all of $2.50 for 100 pounds of picked cotton, and at breakneck speed it takes a long day, much more than eight hours, to pick 150 pounds. Virtually every Negro high school and college graduate in Monroe has to leave to find employment. This is not true of the white graduates. Negroes are even laid off in the summer so the white college youth can work at home. Meanwhile, each summer our street corners are crowded with colored youths just out of school. They have no means of gainful employment nor wholesome recreation.

For reasons such as these we believe that the basic ill is an economic ill; our being denied the right to have a decent standard of living.

The Freedom Riders Come to Monroe

We had planned to put picket lines around the county courthouse to draw attention to our program and to put pressure for its achievement. At this time seventeen Freedom Riders came to our support, perhaps the first time that they engaged in a struggle over such fundamental demands as our program presented. Hitherto, as I've said, the goals were peripheral, and while important, amenable to small compromises. For example, we had won integration in the public library. On these peripheral matters, leaders of the Sit-In Movements can meet with city and state officials and win concessions. I believe this is an important part of the overall Negro struggle, but when these concessions are used for propaganda by Negro "leaders" as examples of the marvelous progress the Afro-American is supposedly making, and thereby shift attention from the basic evils, then such victories cease to be even peripheral and become self-defeating. But when we tackle basic evils, then the racists won't give an inch and this is why, I think, the Freedom Riders who came to Monroe met with such naked violence and brutality. That, and the pledge of non-violence.

77

The Freedom Riders reflected an attitude of certain Negro leaders who had said that I had mishandled the situation and they would show us how to get victory without violence. With them came the Reverend Paul Brooks, sent by the Reverend Martin Luther King, Jr., to act as a "troubleshooter" for the Freedom Riders, should the need arise, and to work with the community, helping them to develop nonviolent techniques and tactics. I disagreed with their position but was more than willing to co-operate. The community rented a house for them which was christened "Freedom House" in their honor. They were joined by some of our militant youth who had participated in the picket lines around the swimming pool the previous month. Together they formed the Monroe Non-Violent Action Committee.

Although I myself would not take the non-violent oath, I asked the people of the community to support them and their non-violent campaign. Monroe students took the non-violent oath, promising to adhere to the non-violent discipline, which, along with other principles, prohibited self-defense. I also stated that if they could show me any gains from the racists by non-violent methods, I too would become a pacifist.

At the same time, several observers were in Monroe to see for themselves what so-called democracy was like in Union County. We knew that people living in other sections of the country, other countries of the world, would find it hard to believe that such vicious racist conditions, such brutality and ruthlessness existed in the United States, especially in such a "progressive" Southern state as North Carolina was supposed to be; so we encouraged these visits. Julian Mayfield, the young Afro-American novelist and an old friend of Monroe, was there. A young exchange student, Constance Lever of Durham, England, was a guest at our house along with Mrs. Mae Mallory, who had been active in the movement for true integration in her own city, New York.

When the Monroe Non-Violent Action Committee set up its picket line, on the first day, the Freedom Riders seemed convinced they were making real progress. One Freedom Rider even returned from the line overjoyed. He said, "You know, a policeman smiled at me in town today while I was on the line." I laughed and told him not to pay that any attention because the policeman was probably smiling at the thought of how best to kill him. Constance, the English exchange student, had joined the picket line and she said, "Oh, I don't think these people are so bad. I just think you don't know how to approach them. I noticed that they looked at me in a friendly way in town today." I tried to explain to her that these people were trying to win her and the others over in the hope that they would leave Monroe. And the day these people realized that they couldn't win the Freedom Riders over, then they would show their true nature. A few days later, Constance Lever was arrested by the Monroe police; and she was charged with "incitement to riot."

The Racists Act by Violence

It was on the third day that the townspeople started insulting the pickets, and their politeness turned to viciousness. A policeman knocked one picket to the ground and threatened to break his camera. Another was arrested. And all the time the white crowd heckled; and when one of the white Freedom Riders smiled back at the hecklers, two of Monroe's "pure white flowers" spit in his face. Tension continued to mount.

On the fourth day, a white Freedom Rider was attacked on the street in town and was beaten by three whites. The police broke this up and promised to arrest the white people who had attacked this Freedom Rider. So the Freedom Riders kept on thinking there was a possibility that the law would be on their side because they had publicly proclaimed themselves to be non-violent. I told them it was all right for them to be pacifists, but they shouldn't proclaim this to the world because they were just inviting full-scale violent attack. In the past we hadn't had any victims of the type of violence they were beginning to experience because we had shown a willingness to fight. We had had picket lines and sit-ins and nobody had successfully attacked our lines. But they said they were struggling from a moral point of view.

On Friday a white Freedom Fighter was shot in the stomach with a high-powered air rifle, as he was walking the line. This happened right in front of the police. And that day the city sprayed the picket line with insecticide, hoping to drive the students away from the line. Meanwhile, the city had passed special laws, ordering pickets to be fifteen feet apart at all times. They had to maintain this distance; they couldn't be too close or too far apart. Then the police started using the tactic of stopping one picket and when the one behind continued walking on they would arrest him for passing too closely behind the other. Also that afternoon, a Negro boy, ten years old, was attacked in town by three white men because he had been seen on the picket line. None of the attackers was arrested.

"Ain't You Dead Yet?"

That night the Freedom Riders went for a ride into Macklenberg County across the line and they stopped at a restaurant. There they were recognized and attacked by white racists. In the scramble, one of the Freedom Riders could escape only by running into the woods; and the others had to flee in the car, leaving him behind. We notified the Monroe city police, our county police, the Charlotte police, and the Macklenberg County police that a Freedom Rider was in the woods, missing, and the racists were trying to catch him. We were afraid he would be lynched. We asked them to intercede. The Monroe police refused. The Union County police refused.

Then Rev. Brooks called the Governor's office. Governor Terry Sanford was out, they said. But Rev. Brooks got an opportunity to speak to the Governor's chief aide, Hugh B. Cannon, and he complained to him about the lack of police protection for the Freedom Riders. The Governor's aide kept talking about Robert Williams. Rev. Brooks said he was not calling about Robert Williams, he was calling about a missing Freedom Rider. He said that they were pacifists; they were non-violent people and they wanted police protection. And the Governor's aide, Hugh B. Cannon, said, "If you're a real pacifist you had better get the hell out of Monroe, man, because there's going to be plenty of violence there."

Rev. Brooks kept trying to appeal to him for police protection but finally he gave up. And he said, "Since you're talking about Robert Williams so much, he's right here. Do you want to talk to him?" The Governor's aide said, Yes.

We had talked about two weeks before when I had asked for state police protection. Instead the Governor had sent an Uncle Tom representative named Dr. Larkins, who is supposed to be the Governor's troubleshooter. He came and held a secret meeting with me to find out what it would take to quiet things down. I gave him the ten-point program and it shocked him. He said that it was too much, that the demands were too high, but he would take it up with the Governor anyway. And he said that, well, he understood I had been undergoing economic pressure and that this was wrong and that maybe I could get a job, that maybe the state could help me if we just didn't start any trouble around here.

When I called back the Governor's office and told Hugh B. Cannon about this bribe attempt, he replied, "You mean to tell me that you're not dead yet?" And I told him, "No, I'm not dead, not yet, but when I die a lot of people may die with me." So he said, "Well, you may not be dead, but you're going to get killed." I kept telling him that we wanted protection, trying to avoid bloodshed. He said, "If you're trying to avoid bloodshed you shouldn't be agitating."

The Governor and the FBI

So this Friday night, when Rev. Paul Brooks finished talking to Hugh B. Cannon and he said he wanted to talk to me, I got on the phone and told him what had happened. He said, "Well, you're getting just what you deserve down there. You've been asking for violence, now you're getting it." I told him that I wasn't appealing to him for myself. I was appealing to him for a pacifist. And I told him, "Besides, I'm not appealing to you for a Negro; this happens to be a white boy who's lost in the woods." He said, "I don't give a damn who he is. You asked for violence and now you're getting it, see; you're getting just what you deserved." So I told him, "Do you know one thing . . . you are the biggest fool in the whole world!" He became infuriated and he started raging on the telephone and he told me to shut up. I told him that he may be the Governor's assistant, but he couldn't tell me to shut up. And he said, "If you don't stop talking to me like that I'll hang up." And he finally hung up. No protection came.

Each time the Freedom Riders would get ready to go on the picket line they would call the FBI in Charlotte asking for protection. The FBI would say, "We're on our way." But they would never be there when anything happened. On Saturday when the Freedom Riders were picketing in town and the taxicabs that had been transporting them to the line had started out to pick them up, the local white racists gathered together and blocked the road. This meant the Freedom Riders had to walk back to the colored community, which was almost a mile away. The mob followed the Freedom Riders along the streets, threw stones at them, and threatened to kill them. When they came into the colored community, the colored people who were not participating in the picket line became very upset that our community had been invaded by a mob chasing Freedom Riders. Many of the colored people started stoning cars and beating back the white racists.

82

Chapter 5

SELF-DEFENSE PREVENTS A POGROM: RACISTS ENGINEER A KIDNAPPING FRAMEUP

Sunday morning the chief of police and his men drove through the county urging whites to come to town to fight the Freedom Riders. In addition, people were coming in from other counties and from South Carolina. And an organization called the Minute Men had brought people in.

By afternoon thousands of white racists had gathered in town, concentrating at the courthouse square. At 4 o'clock James Foreman, one of the picket captains, called my home requesting four taxicabs within the hour. He said the racists were threatening to assault the line, and he complained of police indifference. Foreman was to end up in jail with a split head one hour later.

At 4:30 the Negro cab company called to report that they couldn't get through to the picketers because every entrance into town was blocked off. Minutes later a couple of cars driven by our people came racing into the neighborhood. They had just made it in from town to report that the mob had started to attack the picket line, that shots had been fired, and the town was in the grip of a full-scale riot.

When the self-defense guard, which up to now had stayed away from the courthouse square, heard that the lives of the Freedom Riders and local non-violent youth were in danger, they jumped into their cars and rode into town, breaking through the mob's blockade to rescue the picketers. Julian Mayfield went with them.

The white mob was already armed. Then the police disarmed some of the men attempting to rescue the Freedom Riders, and these additional weapons were turned over to the mob. Firing broke out at the picket line when

83

the police and the mob tried to prevent the English exchange student from getting into one of the rescue cars driven by three armed Negroes. The police held Negroes while white racists beat them up. At first the victims were all Freedom Riders and the local non-violent students, but soon Negroes were attacked indiscriminately as the mob fanned out all over town. They were massing for an attack against our community.

We Aim for Self-Defense

So many Freedom Riders and Negroes were arrested that many prisoners with legitimate charges against them were released from jail to make room. Many of these people who came out of jail reported to me that students were bleeding to death there without any medical attention. I called the chief of police and I told him that I had reports that the students were not getting medical attention and that their lives were in danger. I told him I would give him just thirty minutes to get medical attention for them. That if they didn't receive medical aid within thirty minutes, we would march on the jail. About fifteen minutes later James Foreman called from the hospital to let me know that they were receiving medical care. Just after that, Julian Mayfield returned and reported that members of the white mob, which now included some uniformed police, were near the railroad tracks and firing down at Negroes who had fled town. Just at the beginning of darkness, white people started driving through our community, and they were shouting and screaming and some would fire out of their cars and throw objects at people on the streets. Many of the colored people started arming, exchanging guns and borrowing ammunition and forming guards for the night to defend the community from the mob massing in town. On the block where I live there were about 300 people milling around the street.

About 6 o'clock in the evening a white couple, Mr. and Mrs. Bruce Stegall, came riding through our neighborhood.

The Stegalls were recognized as people who had driven through town the day before with a racist banner on their car. Their banner carried a slogan announcing an "Open Season On Coons." It meant that this was killing time.

People have asked why a racist would take his wife into a riot-torn community like ours on that Sunday. But this is nothing new to those who know the nature of Klan raiding. Many Southern racists consider white women a form of insulation because of the old tradition that a Negro is supposed to be intimidated by a white woman and will not dare to offend her. White women are taken along on Klan raids and if anything develops into a fight it will appear that the Negro attacked a woman and the Klansman will of course be her protector. Mrs. Stegall was brought along as insulation by her husband. They were trying to see what defenses we were preparing for that night.

The Negroes out on the street were raging. Some of them had been beaten in town. Some of their children were missing and some of their children were in jail. As soon as the Stegalls' car entered our street it was recognized and stopped at gunpoint less than a block away from my house. I was in the house at the time receiving telephone calls from all over town: calls from parents crying about their children who had participated in this demonstration; calls from Negroes reporting that they were beaten and asking what should be done, what action to take; calls from Negroes volunteering to fight, Negroes offering to join in armed groups so they could defend the community. When I wasn't on the phone I was out in the back of my house setting up a defense line before nightfall.

When the Stegalls were stopped, they were taken out of their car and brought into my yard. Someone called me out of the house and I came out and saw all these people milling around the Stegalls. I realized how angry these people were and I saw that the circle was closing in around the Stegalls. I knew that if just one person lost control of himself the Stegalls would be killed. I started driving the crowd away from them; forcing the crowd out of reach.

Then Mrs. Stegall said, "We've been kidnapped!" She kept repeating this. I said, "Lady, you're not kidnapped. You can leave when you get ready but you got to go through this crowd and these people are angry." She stood up and looked at the crowd and she said, "You should take us out of here. You could take us out. If you took us out of here they wouldn't bother us." I said, "Lady, I didn't bring you here and I'm not going to take you away. You knew that all these people would be here; you know how rioting has been going on in the town and you should have known better than to come into a place like this where the people are angry and upset like this. We are too busy now trying to defend our homes. I'm trying to set up a defense line and I don't have time to bother with you. That's your problem."

While we were standing there talking, an airplane flew over us. The airplane probably was either from the Klan or the Sheriff's Department. They use plenty of light planes and we were constantly getting calls threatening to bomb us from the air since my house was too well guarded to get us from the ground. So when this plane swooped over the house about fifteen men armed with high-powered .30-caliber rifles opened fire. Mrs. Stegall had been very indignant and arrogant, but as soon as she saw this she realized how serious was the situation; that these people were angry and really meant business. She started shaking all over and she almost became hysterical. Then a car with white men drove by, firing, and about twenty fellows fired back and you could see flames where the bullets struck the car. And Mrs. Stegall could see this.

I started into the house and the crowd began screaming that the Stegalls should be killed. When I started walking up the front steps Mrs. Stegall was right up against me, walking right up against my body and her husband was right up against her. They followed me on into the house while all these people were still screaming that they should be killed, and one man was begging for somebody to give him a gun and let him, please, let him kill them.

Some of the people in this crowd I had never seen before. Negroes were coming from out of the county, they were coming from other towns or calling long-distance on the telephone offering to join in the defense group that was being formed. But all of the people who had been regularly affiliated with me and in the guard were in the back of my house because that was where we were assembling and checking out our weapons and ammunition for the night. The street crowd consisted of Negroes who had become angry and involved. They didn't belong to any organization, to any one group. They were just armed private citizens who were fed up with oppression.

I went to the telephone and my wife gave the Stegalls a seat. When I came back the woman kept repeating, "If you'll take us out of here we'll be all right." And I told her again that I didn't have time to take her out. I told her that if I had been caught in her community under similar conditions I would already be dead. I said, "You see, we are not half as cruel as your people." And she admitted that I was right. She told me that she was a church-going Christian and that she wanted to help us and she wished there was something she could do. And I told her that her husband could help us. And he said he didn't know what he could do since he wasn't well known around Monroe, that they lived in Marshall. She kept saying, "*You're* Robert Williams!" and I told her, Yes. She said, "Well, I never met you before, but I heard a lot of talk about you." And I said, "It was all bad." And she said, "Yes, I must admit that it was all bad, but you're not the type of fellow they say you are. You seem to be a good fellow. You're much better than I thought."

The telephone rang again. It was the chief of police, A. A. Mauney. He said, "Robert, you've caused a lot of race trouble in this town, but state troopers are coming. In thirty minutes you'll be hanging in the courthouse square."

He hung up. Someone else called and said there was a news flash on television that troops were being sent to surround the town. Another woman called and said that she saw troops moving in and that the highway patrol was parking its cars behind the jailhouse. This was confirmed by a radio flash. Then one of our fellows called me to the door. I went out and into the street. I looked around. Both ends were being blocked off by police cars. I realized they were trying to trap me into waiting until the state troopers got there. I told Mabel, my wife, that we had to leave. I said she didn't have time to take anything, just to get the children. I called Julian Mayfield who had left just after the Stegalls followed me in. I told him about the state troopers moving in around my area and advised him to leave Monroe immediately so that if something happened to me, someone would be free to tell the world the story. Then we left.

In Flight But Not a Fugitive

Most people think that we left because we were fleeing an indictment. But the possibility of an indictment hadn't even occurred to me at that time. Remember, I left Monroe knowing I had *saved* the lives of the Stegalls. We were fleeing because of the attitude of the state, because of the attitude of the chief of police; because of the *lack* of law. We didn't learn about the indictment until we were in New York and heard it flashed on radio and television. When we left North Carolina we headed directly for New York. In the beginning I thought that we would stay there; that we would stop over in Harlem and from there we would immediately start a campaign to tell the world about the ruthless racist oppression that was taking place in Monroe. It was for this reason that I had left North Carolina; because only from outside the state could I focus a publicity campaign that would bring help to the Negroes and Freedom Riders so hopelessly outnumbered in Monroe. I had left North Carolina only after the chief of police had called me and told me that the state troopers were coming and that in thirty minutes I would be hanging in the court house square. And I remembered the words of Hugh B. Cannon when I had appealed to him for protection under law for the missing Freedom Rider. The Governor's aide told me that he didn't give a damn about anyone; that we had asked for violence and now we were going to get it. He wanted to know then "why I wasn't dead yet!" I didn't think then anything legal was involved.

The first I knew of the indictment was in New York when I heard over the radio that there was an all-points alarm out for me and that I had been indicted for kidnapping the Stegalls by the Union County Grand Jury.

The FBI claims that it entered the case because I was an indicted fugitive from justice in interstate flight to avoid prosecution. But technically the FBI is wrong, because I left Monroe early that night—about 9 o'clock—and when the grand jury indicted me sometime late the next day, I was already in New York. I certainly didn't cross the North Carolina state line as an indicted fugitive.

But this technical error in the Federal charge that was made against me so that I might be "legally" hounded throughout the whole United States is not at all surprising when one thinks of the complete falsity of the state kidnapping charge. It is very important to note what happened immediately after I left Monroe. I was indicted on the testimony of two policemen (there is no court record that the Stegalls ever appeared before the grand jury). Then, with the warrant issued, my house was raided by about a hundred officials of the state, the Federal government, and the local police armed with machine guns, rifles, riotguns, and tear gas. They didn't know that I had already left. They couldn't believe that I had got away.

When I read about the grand jury indictment in the New York papers it was accompanied by interviews reporters had had with Mrs. Stegall. I don't know what Mrs.

Stegall finally told the grand jury, if she ever did appear before them, but I do know she couldn't keep her story straight for the reporters; and she never did tell the same version twice.

I read stories in *The New York Post* and *The New York Times* the following day reporting that when they had questioned Mrs. Stegall she said that I had chided the crowd for kidnapping her and her husband. Yet she turned around in the next paragraph and said that I was responsible because I was the ringleader of these people. Then the next thing I read was that she claimed that they had been tied up in my house and held at gunpoint and that when I left the house they were still there. But after saying that they were tied up, then she turned around and said that they were released by me unharmed and left an hour and a half later.

Meanwhile, she was claiming various reasons for being in the colored community in the first place. In one paper she said they were taking a short cut; for another paper she said that they were lost, that they didn't know where they were going. But no highway runs through our community. This was a dead-end street almost a mile from the highway that the Stegalls would use to get back to Marshville. Any person who knew the county could not possibly get lost there. And the Stegall woman also told one reporter that the house I lived in, the house that I was born in, had been sold to my father by her father and that she had once lived there herself. Now, in all these stories it was always Mrs. Stegall who was doing the talking and Mrs. Stegall's picture that you would see. They never had Mr. Stegall, who was a known Klansman, say much at all.

I also read a report where Mrs. Stegall was quoted by the *Charlotte Observer* as saying "that Williams only pretended that he was trying to help us." Well, how would she know? One of the best proofs that I must have been helping them is the fact that they're unharmed and still alive. And they know this.

Chapter 6

THE MONROE CASE:
CONSPIRACY AGAINST THE NEGRO

What has happened and continues to happen in Monroe, N.C., illustrates an old truth—that words used in common by all men do not always have a meaning common to all men. Men have engaged in life-or-death struggles because of differences of meaning in a commonly held word. The white racist *believes* in "freedom," he *believes* in "fair trial," he *believes* in "justice." He sincerely believes in these words and can use them with great emotion because to the white racist they mean his freedom to deprive Negroes of their basic human rights, and his courts where a "fair trial" is that procedure, and "justice" that decision which upholds the racist's mad ideal of white supremacy. On many desperate occasions when our constitutional rights were denied and our lives were in danger, we called on the Justice Department and the FBI to investigate the Monroe situation, and to protect our lives and restore our constitutional rights—in other words, *to administer justice*. And they always refused our request.

*The Department of Justice—"Extremely
Dangerous and Schizophrenic"*

The U.S. Justice Department is showing itself as abetting the conspiracy in Monroe against Negroes as the Ku Klux Klan. After we had left Monroe the U.S. Justice Department, in collaboration with the chief of police, A. A. Mauney, released 250,000 "wanted" circulars and in these circulars they described me as being schizophrenic. In describing me as schizophrenic they failed to tell who had psychoanalyzed me. Do they mean I was analyzed as being schizophrenic by Monroe's semi-illiterate chief of police?

91

The Justice Department released these vicious posters that said I was "extremely dangerous." But they failed to cite any substantiating facts. They failed to cite any criminal record. They failed to cite any cases that could justify this charge. They failed to tell what harm I had ever done to anyone. This was because they knew that these things were lies. Now, how could the Justice Department of the United States do this, how could it mean well? How could it be an impartial investigative body, and then spread such vicious lies throughout the United States without so much as investigating the facts; without so much as investigating the source of these malicious lies?

In their posters were such "facts" as that I had a scar over my right eye, a scar to the left of my nostril, and a scar on my left leg. All of this is untrue, but these ridiculous lies about nonexistent scars create a picture of the "razor-fighting nigger"; of someone "extremely dangerous." All of this means that the U.S. Justice Department has joined forces with the Ku Klux Klan. They were so sure that I would not escape that they were prematurely justifying what they considered was going to be a legal lynching at the behest of the United States government. They had said I would not hesitate to shoot. This was to justify someone shooting me if I had been taken into custody.

When I fled to Canada they also passed these same posters on to the Royal Canadian Mounted Police. And in Canada, interestingly enough, they never mentioned the fact that race incidents had occurred in North Carolina. That the only crime that I was guilty of was the crime of fighting for human rights in the South. And this is surely a crime; surely considered a crime in the South for a Negro to fight for his human rights. There is plenty of proof of this. Since the sit-in demonstrations started in the South, over 5,000 Negroes have been arrested for struggling for their rights. Almost all of the militant leaders in the South have spent some time in jail for no more than asking for their Constitutional and human rights.

The Justice Department was afraid that the Canadians, who are not as prejudiced as white Americans, would understand what this case was really all about and refuse to cooperate. They had to make it appear—and this is the work of the United States government through its agency, the U.S. Justice Department—that I was a common criminal who had kidnapped for ransom. They created the impression that I was hiding in Canada and was heavily armed.

Again the question is: *Where did this information come from?* Did the U.S. Justice Department go to the same chief of police that I had asked them to indict? The same chief of police against whom I had filed an affidavit? The same chief of police that they knew had been my enemy and the enemy of Negroes and a friend of the Ku Klux Klan since 1956? Did they go to a Klan-sponsored chief of police to ask him for data on a United States civil rights fighter? Well, they most certainly did. And this should be enough to awaken many people to the fact that the Justice Department of the United States is itself contaminated by racist influences.

If I had not been able to escape from the United States I would never have gotten to a trial, not even to mention a fair trial.

*   *   *

The Other Defendants

Mrs. Stegall reported that my home was an "armed camp." But the raid on my house had failed to produce any trace of these arms or ammunition. So the police used my disappearance as an excuse to raid through the rest of the community; tearing up homes, terrorizing a lot of the people who weren't even in the defense guard, grilling in all-night sessions persons known to be my associates, and

93

confiscating the weapons they found—weapons we possessed legally.

The Freedom Riders who were out of jail said that although I was gone they were going to carry on the struggle; they would carry on this fight that we had started. They made this statement to *The New York Post* and to *The New York Times* a day after I left. One of them was John Lowry, a twenty-year-old white college student from New York. Two days after he declared that the struggle would be continued he was arrested and charged with complicity. Richard Crowder, a local nineteen-year-old youth who had been elected chairman of the Monroe Non-Violent Action Committee, was also indicted along with seventeen-year-old Harold Reape. These boys had participated in the original picket line and in the sit-in demonstration and they had shown leadership ability in this struggle; therefore they were indicted for complicity. Mae Mallory, who left North Carolina after the rioting started, was also charged with complicity, but no immediate attempt was made to apprehend her.

In addition, Albert Rurie (seventeen years old) and Jimmie Covington (fifteen years old), two other local Negro youth who had participated in all of these struggles, were each charged and indicted with having shot a policeman apiece, although the City of Monroe never could produce more than one wounded policeman. Jimmie Covington was committed to reform school. Albert Rurie was given five years in prison. This case is pending on appeal to the state Supreme Court.

Richard Griswold of Brooklyn, New York, another white Freedom Rider arrested during the rioting on the 27th, was beaten almost to the point of death in the Union County jail that day by another prisoner, a white criminal being held on forgery and assault charges. Griswold's life was saved only because another arrested Freedom Rider was led past the cell in which Griswold was lying, blood-covered and semi-conscious. The second Freedom Rider,

Kenneth Shilman, started yelling at the top of his lungs, demanding that Griswold be removed from the cell before he was killed. The warden complied because he thought the white student would die and then there would really be trouble.

Starting the very next day, all the different city, county, state, and Federal law-enforcement agencies began sending each other telegrams about how law and order had been re-established in Monroe. And the week following the riots each employee of the Sheriff's Department was awarded $100 extra pay by the Board of County Commissioners. The bonus was "compensation for special services rendered during the 'race emergencies' in Monroe."

Almost three weeks later The Committee to Aid The Monroe Defendants received a handwritten, signed confession from Howard Stack, the white prisoner who had been Griswald's cellmate. Stack admitted that he had beaten Griswald at the behest of the Monroe police, who had promised to drop the charges against him and release him immediately in exchange for the beating. Stack sent this confession to the CAMD because two weeks after he was released he was again picked up and sentenced on the same charges that were supposedly dropped.

Conrad Lynn forwarded the original of the confession to Attorney General Robert Kennedy and asked for an immediate investigation of the Monroe Police Department. The Justice Department never acknowledged receiving the confession. FBI agents did come around and secure depositions and they even interviewed Stack. Meanwhile, Union County authorities quickly committed Stack to a mental institution and the Justice Department notified Lynn, finally, that their file was closed.

The Spectre of the Russian Rifles

Soon various newspapers in the United States began to report statements by local police officials that when they raided our community they discovered and seized our

On or about 4th Sunday
of Aug 1961. I was in
the Union County Jail
on 3 charges of worthless
checks and two assault
charges. The Monroe police
and deputy forces of the
City of Monroe put to
me a proposition if I
would let force assault
on of the freedom
riders. Howard they
would set I went
free of my charges. This
bed boy I slept in the
bottom cell in the Union
County Jail. I went free
for 2 week and was
picked back up and sentenced
for the crime which
was supposed to be dropped
for the assault I did
for them they turned
their back on me is
why I confess to this

Howard Stack

Handwritten confession of Howard Stack that he beat up the young Freedom Rider Griswold at the behest of the Monroe police. This confession was sent to the Department of Justice who took no action.

secret armory: *Russian rifles with sickle and hammer insignia.* They implied that these weapons were supplied by some sort of ominous international Communist conspiracy. The insinuation was that of a secret weapons cache shipped to us directly by Moscow. This was a pure smear. They suppressed the information that many of our rifles were of *various* foreign makes. They failed to mention that we had rifles with the insignia of the Crown; British surplus rifles. Why didn't they recognize that we were agents of the Queen, hoping to restore the monarchy in America? Nor did they mention our rifles of Italian manufacture. They failed to mention that we also had German rifles with Nazi insignia. These were World War II weapons, Mausers. It should be noted that they didn't think enough of this to mention that we had such weapons. Possibly they approve of rifles with Nazi insignia. And they failed to mention that we had surplus rifles from the United States Army, the M-1 rifle with U.S. Army insignia. Why didn't they try to involve us in a conspiracy with the U.S. Army?

They only mentioned the rifles of Russian origin in order to smear our self-defense movement. It was a tactic to arouse hysteria among the racists and to mislead the American people. It was an attempt to inject fake emotional issues of the Cold War into our fight for survival. It was an attempt to make the American people think that the Monroe self-defense movement was a grave threat to their security.

The plain fact is that these rifles can be bought in army-navy surplus stores and regular hardware stores throughout the United States. These rifles were purchased legally. Including the Russian rifles with the hammer and sickle insignia. I received signed bills of sale with the numbers of these Russian rifles on them.

This was no special secret supply or hidden armory. We had a rifle club with a charter from the National Rifle

Association since 1957. We were authorized to have rifles. We did target practice. There are three other gun clubs in Monroe, three white gun clubs. The white people even have two segregated professional rifle ranges. But not a single newspaper mentioned any of these facts.

Newspapers like *The New York Post* started crying and sobbing hysterically about Russian rifles being found, but they failed to mention that these rifles were bought openly in stores in the United States. These Russian rifles were not automatic weapons. They were the bolt-action type used for sport and marksmanship firing, and had won five out of six trials in the Olympics of 1959. This rifle is called the 6.53 and it is not even used in the Russian Army. The "Russian rifles" smear was allowed to be perpetrated by sensationalist journalists who somehow didn't see anything at all sensational when policemen armed white thugs to attack non-violent students in Monroe.

I have a picture taken from a recent issue of the *Toronto Star* of members of the so-called U.S. Minute Men, the fascistic organization that is in fellowship with the John Birch Society. The photograph shows the Minute Men in training in the state of Illinois. Not the state of Mississippi, not the state of Alabama or South Carolina, but in the state of Illinois. These people are equipped with machine guns and automatic rifles, including the Johnson automatic rifle, and they are firing U.S. Army 6.5-mm. mortars. They are firing these mortars on prepared ranges and they are firing live ammunition. Where did they get these mortars? Where did they get this ammunition? No surplus stores in the United States sell mortars or live shells. Where did they get their machine guns and automatic rifles, many of the models of which still are in use by the United States Armed Forces? Unlike our weapons, automatic rifles and machine guns may not be owned by civilians; this is specified by Federal law.

These men are wearing standard steel helmets and they are dressed in surplus uniforms of the U.S. Army. The only difference is that they have their own Minute Men insignia. These men have raised and mobilized their own private army; and a part of the 5,000 men recruited in Monroe to attack the Freedom Riders were components of this fascistic Minute Men organization.

Nobody was upset about this. None of these pious-sounding newspapers, so much interested in the welfare and the security of the American people, breathed a word about Minute Men being brought into Monroe. These Minute Men have been arming and training with heavy weapons in the field. What is the reason for this? Why has this been tolerated in the United States? The Minute Men say that they are mobilizing to fight Communism or possible invasion of the United States by the Communists. Wouldn't an American be naive indeed to believe that if the United States Marine Corps, and the Infantry, and the Navy, and the Air Force couldn't stop some sort of invasion, how in the hell could a few old women in tennis shoes from the John Birch Society and their corps of Minute Men stop them?

No. Anyone who can think logically can see that the racist Minute Men are being armed and prepared for pogroms. They are becoming a fascist vanguard that will some day be turned loose on all Afro-Americans and white Americans who get out of line. And to get out of line means to petition militantly for Constitutional rights. These Minute Men types will be the people who do the dirty work. Just as there were special units to man the gas furnaces for the Jewish people in Nazi Germany, so "special units" will develop to handle "trouble-makers" in a fascist America. This must be done outside of the jurisdiction of the armed forces because the U.S. Armed Services are integrated. But the Minute Men organizations are not integrated. It will be like the French Army and the O.A.S. in Algeria. They will look the other way, like the Wehrmacht and the S.S. corps in Hitler's time. The Armed Services of the United States, the police officials, the Justice

99

Department will look the other way and they will say, "We're sorry, but we can't catch these people. We're sorry, but we've done everything we can do to prevent violence." The Minute Men have pure, 100 per cent, all-American weapons and the newspapers have barely found cause to denounce their activities.

But when the Negroes of Monroe, outnumbered and outarmed, gallantly rose to defend their homes, their families, and their persons, their efforts at self-defense were scorned by the press and they were smeared with the insinuation that their weapons were furnished by some insidious Communist conspiracy.

All of the American people, not just the Afro-Americans, must realize that if we had not been armed in this city of Monroe, Union County, North Carolina, last August 27, there would have been mass bloodshed. There is only one reason why the racist mob lost its nerve in their projected attack on the Negro community. Knowing as they did that we were well armed, they found it impossible to stomach the thought of violence.

These are people who would like to do violence to others but want to have immunity from violence themselves. They are the people who just love it when pacifist Negroes turn the other cheek.

Our preparations and constant armed vigilance to protect our homes from attack were completely divorced from the campaign of the Freedom Riders and our local students who were picketing and demonstrating on a non-violent basis. *We armed ourselves solely to defend ourselves.* And if we hadn't been armed we would have been the victims of one of the first modern pogroms against the Afro-American. Let the newspapers wail and bemoan about our rifles with Communist insignia. I don't care what kind of insignias the rifles had on them. They were a godsend to us that Sunday, August 27, 1961.

100

When I realized that this was no longer a local matter; that the U.S. Government had entered into the picture and was just as determined to destroy me as the Ku Klux Klan, I decided that I had to leave New York and that the best place to go would be Canada.

I felt that the Canadian people would be sympathetic. I also remembered that Canada had been a place of refuge for escaped Negroes using the underground railway during the time of slavery in the United States. So I made my way on to Canada and my wife Mabel was there with me. I felt secure in Canada. For a few days I lived a normal life. I went around town shopping—window shopping; I attended an air show and I went to the park and to the beaches. It seemed to me that I was quite secure. I felt that there was a possibility that I would be able to remain in Canada since charges against me were really trumped up.

One morning, to my surprise, there was a huge picture of me on the front page of a Canadian newspaper. The story that went with the photo said that I was a vicious kidnapper and that the Justice Department of the United States had appealed to the Royal Canadian Mounted Police to apprehend me. It referred to me as being a laborer and a freight handler. It didn't mention the fact that I was president of the Union County branch of the National Association for the Advancement of Colored People. Nor did it mention that I had written, edited, and published a newsletter.

The Royal Canadian Mounted Police initiated a search that was just as vicious and carried out just as energetically as the FBI search. Since there were many Canadians who realized what the race situation was in the United States and who sympathized with me, the Royal Canadian Mounted Police started searching homes. They even searched a church in Toronto (and questioned the minister) where I had appeared while on a speaking tour the

Robert F. Williams at a press conference with the Cuban Bar Association, March 1962 (photo by LeRoy McLucas).

THE CRUSADER

MONTHLY NEWSLETTER

ROBERT F. WILLIAMS, EDITOR   —IN EXILE—

VOL. 3 — No. 8   APRIL 1962

Truth Crushed to Earth Shall Rise Again

IT has truly been said that "truth crushed to earth shall rise again." True to this adage, the fighting little CRUSADER Newsletter returns to the vanguard of the

CUBA: TERRITORIO LIBRE DE AMÉRICA

liberation struggle. Yes, it yet lives to haunt those who thought they had destroyed it. THE CRUSADER with its editor in exile is going to be a monthly printed journal. It

previous summer. I decided that Canada would be no safer than the United States. I had made plans with sympathetic Canadians to fight extradition proceedings if I was apprehended in Canada. They were prepared to show that the authorities were trying to return me to the violence, brutality, and racial oppression of the South, and they had hired lawyers for me in Canada who were ready to take immediate legal action in the event of my arrest. But luckily I was able to leave Canada.

When I realized that I would not be safe in Canada, I remembered my two trips to Cuba. I could think of no other place in the Western Hemisphere than Cuba where a Negro would be treated as a human being; where the race problem would be understood; and where people would not look upon me as a criminal, but as a victim of a trumped-up charge—a charge designed to crush the militant leaders who were beginning to form a new movement, a new militant movement designed for the total liberation of the Afro-Americans.

Since all of the eastern coast of Canada was being watched by the FBI and the Royal Canadian Mounted Police, I traveled across Canada to the west coast, re-entered the United States and made my way into Mexico and from there to Cuba. That was why I came to Cuba; because I had no alternative.

*　　*　　*

The Complicity of the Ohio Governor

Shortly after Cuba announced that she had granted me political asylum, Mrs. Mae Mallory was arrested by agents of the FBI in Cleveland, Ohio, where she had gone for asylum. The state of North Carolina immediately requested that she be extradited back to Union County to stand trial.

If Mrs. Mallory is extradited, she will join Lowry, Reape, and Crowder and be tried on a yet undetermined date in a North Carolina court, where there is no possible chance of their obtaining justice; especially under the conditions that I've described. Much pressure is building up throughout the country; many people are preparing to protest this great miscarriage of justice, for these indictments carry lifetime sentences in prison.

When Mrs. Mallory was first arrested in Cleveland considerable protest occurred in Ohio. Responding to this pressure by the Afro-American community, the Rev. Martin Luther King Jr. signed a Monroe Defense Committee petition asking Gov. Michael DiSalle not to extradite Mae Mallory. Mrs. Mallory was granted an executive hearing and two months later Gov. DiSalle made his decision. It was to extradite Mrs. Mallory back to Monroe.

Despite thousands of petition signatures, telegrams, and letters of protest from trade unions, civil liberties organizations, and civic groups not only in Cleveland but throughout the country, Gov. DiSalle made this decision and refused to reverse it. Gov. DiSalle justified his decision on the basis of two telephone conversations with North Carolina's Gov. Terry Sanford, who "assured" Gov. DiSalle that "Mrs. Mallory would receive a fair trial in a North Carolina court."

Does this great liberal Governor of Ohio really believe Negroes can secure justice in North Carolina courts just because the Governor of that state assured him that such justice exists? North Carolina is a state where a Negro man was convicted and sentenced to five years in prison because it was said that he leered at a white woman; that he looked at her too attentively. Despite the fact that he was 75 feet away, he was still convicted in a state superior court, and sentenced to five years.

This is also a state where just two years ago a seventeen-year-old Negro girl was beaten to death in prison; beaten to death by a guard because she complained about the bad prison food. The state entered into a settlement with her parents. They paid her parents $1,900 as a settlement for having killed their daughter.

Evidently this is Gov. DiSalle's concept of "assured" justice for Negroes. Does he find even more reassuring the instances of so-called North Carolina "justice" that have occurred since the August frame-ups?

This is a state where in early fall, while Gov. DiSalle was talking over the phone with Gov. Terry Sanford and "carefully examining the North Carolina record in administered justice," a young girl, a Negro teen-ager, raped by four white men she could positively identify, was unable to obtain justice from any North Carolina law enforcement agency. When she went to the Marshville police, and the Union County sheriff's office, and finally to the FBI and told them that she had been raped and told them the names of the men who had raped her, all refused to do anything about it. The local FBI office refused because they said this was a local matter. Then finally, when the pressure from the Negro community threatened to become explosive, one of the men was charged, brought to trial, and in five minutes acquitted.

In this same state, just weeks after Gov. DiSalle made his decision to extradite Mae Mallory, a twenty-year-old Negro was convicted of rape and sentenced to ten to twenty years in prison. Despite the fact that the white woman involved repeatedly asserted in court that it was not he who had raped her, the white jury brought in their verdict of guilty. They did this because they knew that the accused and the woman had been long-time friends—something these people cannot tolerate.

At the same time, in this same state, North Carolina, in this same city, Monroe, another Negro youth, held incommunicado for twenty days on three trumped-up charges, was shot in the leg by a policeman when he attempted to escape from the dungeon cell in which he was being kept in solitary confinement—the same cell in which Richard Griswald was so brutally beaten. No North Carolina attorney would represent this boy, Jayvan Covington. Finally, two young Washington, D.C., lawyers volunteered their

106

services as counsel only a week before the trial was scheduled, but the court refused them more time to prepare the defense. Jayvan Covington was found guilty of three felony charges and he was also convicted on two misdemeanors: resisting arrest—he wanted to know what he had been arrested for—and attempted escape. He was sentenced to seven to ten years on these charges. When an appeal was filed a $15,500 bond was set pending appeal. So Jayvan Covington is still in his cell and recently has been threatened with an extra charge of "secret assault" if he goes through with his appeal.

This is the same law, the same court that set bail at $2,000 for a white man, a known member of the Klan, charged with murder, charged with killing a Negro man by shooting him in the back of the head. This white man doesn't even deny the shooting; he claimed he had caught the Negro peeping into a local joyhouse. A week prior to this, another Negro was shot in the hip and is in serious condition. Yet he is in jail unable to raise the $8,000 bail while the white man who shot him is free—claiming he shot the Negro for attempting to break and enter, or for peeping—the Monroe court hasn't decided yet what to call it so it will sound most believable at trial.

This is North Carolina, the state where the second highest official in the government expressed surprise that I was still alive when we appealed to him for no more than enforcement of law and order. This is what Governor Sanford would like to have Mae Mallory return to; this is the type of justice in store for the Negro youth who are now facing trial there, and for John Lowry.

The Mallory case reminds us once more that no Afro-American is out of the reach of Klan justice so long as he is on soil presided over by racists. It is an indictment of American justice to have a Northern state collaborate with the South in a legal lynching. The Mallory case proves that even a Northern state like Ohio helps the racists. Terry

Sanford knows that he can depend on a fellow Democrat like DiSalle to return fugitive slaves.

*   *   *

To the World: "Take Note of Monroe"

On a date to be fixed after Mae Mallory is returned to North Carolina, my co-defendants will be brought to trial in a Monroe, North Carolina, courtroom. Only an aroused and outraged world opinion can possibly save them from the frame-up fate that the authorities have planned. Only an attentive world opinion, sharply focused on that Monroe courtroom, can possibly restrain the racist authorities.

We are asking the world to take note of Monroe, to register its indignation and shock that a government which proclaims itself leader of the "free world" persecutes its freedom-fighting youth.

We have started a world-wide campaign for signatures to a petition which will be presented to the Human Rights Commission of the United Nations. It demands an immediate international investigation into the denial of human rights in Monroe. We are asking labor organizations, human rights committees, and student organizations all over the world to join in this protest.

Our one hope for the Monroe defendants is that the United States will be civilized enough and responsive enough to be mindful that the whole world is disgusted with its treatment of the Afro-American. We hope that the pressure of world resentment will force the U.S. government to give them justice regardless of their race, regardless of their role as freedom fighters, and regardless of their dissent in a racist system; and that they will be restored to the decent society of people who believe in social justice.

This is not a new tactic. World protest saved two young boys from fourteen-year reformatory sentences in the Monroe "Kissing Case." In 1960, when the Monroe city officials drafted an "urban renewal plan" calling for Federal "slum clearance" funds to condemn and destroy the houses of the colored community, we telegraphed a protest-appeal to honorary NAACP member Pandit Nehru, who at that moment had President Eisenhower as his guest in India. The Federal Housing Administration subsequently refused to approve the Monroe project. In 1961, after the Cuban invasion fiasco, when President Kennedy justified U.S. intervention for "the cause of freedom," we sent an open telegram (read at the United Nations) to the President requesting equivalent U.S. tanks, airplanes, artillery, machine guns, and mercenary troops to fight the Klan in North Carolina.

The only difference now is that we will mobilize opinion on a larger scale. When the racists forced me into exile they unwittingly led me onto a greater field of battle.

This is the time for demonstrations like the one we had in the United Nations protesting the lynching of Patrice Lumumba. We must display the type of courage that will embarrass this nation before the world. All this time we will further identify our struggle for liberation with the struggle of our brothers in Africa, and the struggle of the oppressed of Asia and Latin America. They, in turn will further identify their struggle with ours. The U.S. government is powerful enough to eliminate racial discrimination overnight. But it tolerates and abets Jim Crow.

This government will increasingly discover that every discriminatory action against Afro-Americans it tolerates or abets will be understood as a crime against their brothers by the "uncommitted" colored peoples it so wishes to influence.

Chapter 7

SELF-DEFENSE:
AN AMERICAN TRADITION

The stranglehold of oppression cannot be loosened by
a plea to the oppressor's conscience. Social change in something as fundamental as racist oppression involves violence.
You cannot have progress here without violence and upheaval, because it's struggle for survival for one and a
struggle for liberation for the other. Always the powers
in command are ruthless and unmerciful in defending their
position and their privileges. This is not an abstract rule
to be meditated upon by Americans. This is a truth that
was revealed at the birth of America, and has continued
to be revealed many times in our history. The principle of
self-defense is an American tradition that began at Lexington and Concord.

Minds Warped by Racism

We have come to comprehend the nature of racism. It
is a mass psychosis. When I've described racial conditions
in the United States to audiences of foreign newsmen,
Cubans and other Latin Americans, they have been shocked
to learn of the depths of American race hatred. When I
have cited as illustrations such extreme situations as the
segregation of telephone party-lines in Union County, or
the segregated pet-animal cemetery in Washington, D.C.,
where an Afro-American cannot bury his dog, they find
such things comic as well as pathetic.

Such extreme examples of the racist mentality only appear comic when looked upon as isolated phenomena. In
truth they are perfectly logical applications of the premises
that make up the racist mentality. Look at the phenomena
this way and they are the logical inventions of a thoroughly
diseased mind. The racist is a man crazed by hysteria at

110

the idea of coming into equal human contact with Negroes. And this mass mental illness called racism is very much a part of the "American Way of Life."

When Afro-American liberation is finally achieved in the U.S.A., one of the many new developments in such a society will be some sort of institution that will correct those Americans whose minds are thoroughly warped by racism. Somehow a way will be found so that these insane people will be made whole, will be made well again.

✳   ✳   ✳

"We Must Create a Black Militancy . . ."

This is the time for the Afro-American to act. Our sense of national consciousness and militancy is growing. I speak of the masses of people, the masses of Afro-Americans that I know and have visited; in Jacksonville, Florida; in Atlanta, in Savannah, and in Macon, Georgia; in Columbia, in Charleston, and in Greenville, South Carolina. The oppressed and exploited black men that I've met on the streets of Harlem, on the streets of Detroit, and in Chicago. And I speak of the people in Monroe where five years ago, when I started talking about self-defense, I would walk through the streets and many of my black neighbors would walk away to avoid me. Today, despite the FBI manhunt and my exile, despite the frame-up arrests and the shootings since, despite the intimidation campaigns like the one to drive Mrs. Johnson of *The Crusader* staff from Monroe, despite all of this, black Monroe continues its struggle.

As editor of *The Crusader*, I went south in the fall of 1960, deep into Jim Crowland, to observe the freedom struggle. I was confronted with this new wonderful spirit rising throughout Dixie—this determination to break the chains of bondage and the spirit of valor of a people who just a few years ago were submissive peons in civilization's no-man's-land. Daily, I saw the old myth about Afro-Americans being incapable of unity and action exploded.

In Savannah an NAACP leader had contributed $30,000 to the local branch. The branch has a full-time worker and a suite of office space. Pickets and sit-iners have been beaten, and jobs have been lost, but the struggle goes on. The leader is not afraid of violence to himself because the people are with him. In that city an Afro-American union leader said that it had come to pass that the masses of Afro-Americans can see that "We must defend ourselves against violence with violence." That many of them now say that the American white racist needs a good "whipping" to bring him down to earth and to break his white supremacy mania.

I learned in Atlanta that Mr. Elijah Muhammed had made quite an impression and that many Afro-Americans are learning, to the consternation and embarrassment of the black respectable leadership, that he has more to offer than weak prayers of deliverance. A prominent minister in South Carolina said, "Our biggest stumbling block is the Uncle Tom minister—the people must stop paying these traitors." In Atlanta, a university professor, energetic about the new spirit on the part of the Negroes, was very hopeful that new militant leadership would replace the old Uncle Toms, whose days, he was confident, were numbered.

There are exceptions among us. The Uncle Toms, the Judases, and the Quislings of the black "elite" would deny this rising consciousness. They do everything possible to make white Americans think that it is not true, while apologizing to us for the very people who oppress us. Some of these "responsible" Negroes are afraid that militant action damages "amiable race relations." They complain that race relations may deteriorate to a point that many Negroes may lose jobs. What they mean is that they may lose *their* jobs. For the black workers, who are the first to be fired, and last, if ever, to be hired, the situation is so bad it can't deteriorate.

We realize that there must be a struggle within our own

112

ranks to take the leadership away from the black Quislings who betray us. Then the white liberals who are dumping hundreds of thousands of dollars into our struggle in the South to convert us to pacifism will have to accept *our* understanding of the situation or drop their liberal pretensions.

Why do the white liberals ask us to be non-violent? We are not the aggressors; we have been victimized for over 300 years! Yet nobody spends money to go into the South and ask the racists to be martyrs or pacifists. But they always come to the downtrodden Negroes, who are already oppressed and too submissive as a group, and they ask them not to fight back. There seems to be a pattern of some sort of strange coincidence of interest when whites preach a special doctrine to Negroes. Like the choice of theology when the plantation-owners saw to the Christianization of the slaves. Instead of the doctrines which produced the rugged aggressively independent and justice-seeking spirit that we associate with Colonial America as the New England Conscience, the slaves were indoctrinated in the most submissive "trust-your-master" pie-in-the-sky after-you-die form of Christianity.

It is because our militancy is growing that they spend hundreds of thousands of dollars to convert us into pacifists. Because our militancy is growing they come to us out of fear.

Of course, the respectable Negro leadership are the most outspoken exponents of non-violence. But if these people, especially the ministers, are such pure pacifists, why is it that so few, if any, criticize the war preparations of this country? Why is it that so few speak out against the Bomb? Isn't that the sort of preaching one expects and *hears* from sincere pacifists? The responsible Negro leadership is pacifist in so far as its one interest is that we do not fight white racists; that we do not "provoke" or enrage them. They constantly tell us that if we resort to violent self-defense we will be exterminated. They are not stopping violence—they are only stopping defensive violence against white racists out of a fear of extermination.

This fear of extermination is a myth which we've exposed in Monroe. We did this because we came to have an active understanding of the racist system and we grasped the relationship between violence and racism. The existence of violence is at the very heart of a racist system. The Afro-American militant is a "militant" because he defends himself, his family, his home, and his dignity. He does not *introduce* violence into a racist social system—the violence is already there, and has always been there. It is precisely this unchallenged violence that allows a racist social system to perpetuate itself. When people say that they are opposed to Negroes "resorting to violence" what they really mean is that they are opposed to Negroes defending themselves and challenging the exclusive monopoly of violence practiced by white racists. We have shown in Monroe that with violence working *both ways* constituted law will be more inclined to keep the peace.

When Afro-Americans resist and struggle for their rights they also possess a power greater than that generated by their will and their hands. With the world situation as it is today, the most racist and fascist United States government conceivable could not succeed in exterminating 20,000,000 people. We know there is a great power struggle going on in the world today, and the colored peoples control the true balance of power. We also know, from the statistics of the Detroit race riots, that production in this country would fall in forty-eight hours. People everywhere in the world would be ready to support our struggle.

Nor should we forget that this same deceiving pacifist-preaching well-to-do southern blacks profit from the struggle, living lives of luxury while most Afro-Americans continue to suffer. Are they any better than the Negro Quisling in neighboring Charleston, North Carolina—a black man who rode around in a new pink Cadillac with anti-NAACP and anti-integration literature, a huge roll of money, and an expense account, all the blessings of the White Citizens' Council? It is an ironic sign that black Judases are becoming more expensive as the white racist becomes desperate—though it is a small consolation to those of us who suffer from his betrayals.

In Monroe, where we fought the Klan, we were being penalized. There are children there growing up without any education, children without shoes, children without food. Old people without medical attention. For the Monroe Negro, there is no work; there is no welfare. From all the money raised in the North by the official black leadership, no one would send a penny to Monroe, because the white liberals who gave this money considered us to be outlaws and thugs. They preferred to let us suffer rather than to identify themselves with our position. They sent truck convoys into other places in the South, but penalized us because we took a militant stand.

But our children who are growing up without shoes are also growing up with a sense of direction they cannot obtain in the Jim Crow schools. There once was a threat, in Monroe, of Negro teen-age gang war. It abated as the teen-agers resolved their difficulties by coming to understand the problem. It is only natural to expect the black youth to be infected with a desire to do something. Frustrated by less active adults, this desire may be projected in the wrong direction. The vigor of the youth can be channeled into constructive militant actions. It is simply a matter of common sense to have these young Negroes constructively fight racial injustice rather than fight among themselves. Danger is not a respecter of color lines; it is better to bleed for a just cause than to bleed just for the thrill of the sight of blood. Rebellion ferments in modern youth. It is better that it expend itself against its true enemies than against teen-age schoolmates who can't even explain the reasons for their dangerous skirmishes.

The Montgomery bus boycott was perhaps the most successful example of completely pacifist action. But we must remember that in Montgomery, where Negroes are riding in the front of buses, there are also Negroes who are starving. The Montgomery bus boycott was a victory— but it was limited. It did not raise the Negro standard of living; it did not mean better education for Negro children, it did not mean economic advances.

Just what was the issue at hand for the white racists? What sacrifice? Remember that in Montgomery most of the white Americans have automobiles and are not dependent on the buses. It's just like our own experience in Monroe when we integrated the library. I just called the chairman of the board in my county. I told him that I represented the NAACP, that we wanted to integrate the library, and that our own library had burned down. And he said, "Well, I don't see any reason why you can't use the same library that our people use. It won't make any difference. And after all, I don't read anyway." Now, this is the attitude of a lot of white Southerners about the Montgomery bus boycott. The white people who control the city didn't ride the buses anyway; they had their own private cars, so it didn't make any difference to them.

But when Afro-Americans get into the struggle for the right to live as human beings and the right to earn the same amount of money, then they'll meet the greatest amount of resistance, and out of it will come police-condoned or inspired violence. When that happens, the racist must be made to realize that in attacking us he risks his own life. After all, his life is a white life, and he considers the white life to be superior; so why should he risk a superior life to take an inferior one?

Now I believe, and a lot of other Negroes do too, that we must create a black militancy of our own. We must direct our own struggle, achieve our own destiny. We must realize that many Afro-Americans have become skeptical and extremely suspicious of the so-called white liberals who have dominated "Negro" freedom movements. They just feel that no white person can understand what it's like to be a suppressed Negro. The traditional white liberal leadership in civil rights organizations, and even white radicals, generally cannot understand what our struggle is and how we feel about it. They have always made our struggle secondary and after all these years we really never got any place.

They have a patient sense for good public relations. But we're not interested in a good press. We're interested in becoming free. We want to be liberated. To me, oppression is harmful. It is painful. I would wake up in the morning as a Negro who was oppressed. At lunchtime, I would eat as a Negro who was oppressed. At night, I would go to bed as a Negro who was oppressed. And if I could have been free in thirty seconds, it would not have been too soon.

"Too long have others spoken for us," began the first editorial in the first Afro-American newspaper, which began publication in 1827. The truth of these words has not dimmed in the century and a half since they first appeared in *Freedom's Journal*. They are more appropriate than ever.

There *are* white people who are willing to give us aid without strings attached. They are willing to let us direct our own struggle; they are genuinely interested in the liberation of the Negroes. I wouldn't have been able to remain in the South as long as I did if it had not been for the support that I got from some white people in the North. And I might never have succeeded in escaping the legal-lynching manhunt fomented by the FBI, nor have reached Cuban sanctuary but for the help of whites. They will be willing to continue helping us for the sake of justice, for the sake of human decency.

"Every Freedom Movement in the U.S.A.
Is Labeled 'Communist' "

I'm not a member and I've never been a member of the Communist Party. But most decent-minded Americans should realize by now that every movement for freedom that is initiated in the United States; every movement for

117

human dignity, for decency; every movement that seeks fairness and social justice; every movement for human rights, is branded as "Communistic." Whenever a white person participates in a movement for black liberation, the movement is automatically branded as "under the domination of Moscow." I can't expect to be an exception.

This Communist-thing is becoming an old standard. An old standard accusation now. Anyone who uncompromisingly opposes the racists, anyone who scorns the religious fanatics and the super-duper American conservatives is considered a Communist.

This sort of thing gives the Communists a lot of credit, because certainly many people in my movement in the South don't know what a Communist is. Most of our people have never even heard of Marx. When you say Marx some of the people would think that maybe you were talking about a fountain pen or a New York City cab driver. Or the movie comedians.

But people aspire to be free. People want to be liberated when they are oppressed. No matter where the leadership comes from. The enslavement and suppression of Negroes in the American South were going on before Karl Marx was born, and Negroes have been rebelling against their oppression before Marxism came into existence. As far back as the 16th century, and the beginning of the 17th century, Negroes were even rebelling on the slave ships. The history of American Negro slavery was marked by very many conspiracies and revolts on the part of Negroes.

Certainly the Marxists have participated in the human rights struggle of Negroes, but Negroes need not be told by any philosophy or by any political party that racial oppression is wrong. Racial oppression itself inspires the Negro to rebellion. And it is on this ground that the people of Monroe protested; and on this ground that the people of Monroe refused to conform to the standard of Jim Crow life in a Jim Crow society. It is on this basis that they have struck out against the insanity of racial prejudice. We

118

know that the Southern bigot, the Southern racist is mentally ill; that he is sick. The fact that Jim Crow discrimination and racial segregation may very well be based on economic exploitation is beside the point.

We are oppressed and no matter what the original cause or purpose of this oppression, the mind and personality of the racist doing the oppressing have been warped for so long that he is a mental case. Even if the economic situation is changed it will take quite a while, and it will require quite a shock, to cure this mental disease. I've read that one of the best treatments for some forms of mental illness is the shock treatment. And the shock treatment must come primarily from the Afro-American people themselves in conjunction with their white allies; in conjunction with the white youth.

This movement that I led was not a political organization. It had no political affiliations whatsoever. It was a movement of people who resented oppression. But I would say one thing about our movement. What happened in Monroe, North Carolina, had better become a lesson to the oppressors and the racists of America. Because it is symbolic of a new attitude, symbolic of a new era. It means that the Negro people are becoming restless. It means that there will be many more racial explosions in the days to come. Monroe was just the beginning. I dare predict that Monroe will become the symbol of the new Afro-American; a symbol of the Afro-American determined to rid himself of the stigma of race prejudice and the pain and torture of race hate and oppression at any cost.

Black Nationalism; Another Label

The label Black Nationalist is as meaningless as the Communist label. The Afro-American resents being set aside and oppressed, resents not being allowed to enter the mainstream of American society. These people who form their own groups, because they have been rejected, and start trying to create favorable societies of their own are called "Black Nationalists."

This is a misleading title. Because the first thing you must remember is that *I* am an Afro-American and *I've* been denied the right to enter the mainstream of society in the United States. As an Afro-American I am rejected and discriminated against. We are the most excluded, the most discriminated-against group in the United States; the most discriminated-against class. So it is only normal that I direct most of my energy toward the liberation of my people, who are the most oppressed class.

As for being a "Black Nationalist," this is a word that's hard to define. No, I'm not a "Black Nationalist" to the point that I would exclude whites or that I would discriminate against whites or that I would be prejudiced toward whites. I would prefer to think of myself as an *Inter-Nationalist*. That is, I'm interested in the problems of all mankind. I'm interested in the problems of Africa, of Asia, and of Latin America. I believe that we all have the same struggle; a struggle for liberation. Discrimination and race hatred are undesirable, and I'm just as much against racial discrimination, in all forms, every place in the world, as I am against it in the United States.

What do we mean by "nationalism"? When you consider the present white American society it can be classified as nothing but a nationalistic society based on race. Yet as soon as an Afro-American speaks out for his people, and is conscious and proud of his people's historical roots and culture, he becomes a "nationalist." I don't mind these labels. I don't care what they call me. I believe in justice for all people. And because the Afro-American is the most exploited, the most oppressed in our society, I believe in working foremost for his liberation.

*   *   *

Non-Violence and Self-Defense

The tactics of non-violence will continue and should

120

continue. We too believed in non-violent tactics in Monroe. We've used these tactics; we've used all tactics. But we also believe that any struggle for liberation should be a flexible struggle. We shouldn't take the attitude that one method alone is the way to liberation. This is to become dogmatic. This is to fall into the same sort of dogmatism practiced by some of the religious fanatics. We can't afford to develop this type of attitude.

We must use non-violence as a means as long as this is feasible, but the day will come when conditions become so pronounced that non-violence will be suicidal in itself. The day is surely coming when we will see more violence on the same American scene. The day is surely coming when some of the same Negroes who have denounced our using weapons for self-defense will be arming themselves. There are those who pretend to be horrified by the idea that a black veteran who shouldered arms for the United States would willingly take up weapons to defend his wife, his children, his home, and his life. These same people will one day be the loud advocates of self-defense. When violent racism and fascism strike at their families and their homes, not in a token way but in an all-out bloody campaign, then they will be among the first to advocate self-defense. They will justify their position as a question of survival. When it is no longer some distant Negro who's no more than a statistic, no more than an article in a newspaper; when it is no longer their neighbors, but it means them and it becomes a matter of personal salvation, then will their attitude change.

As a tactic, we use and approve non-violent resistance. But we also believe that a man cannot have human dignity if he allows himself to be abused; to be kicked and beaten to the ground, to allow his wife and children to be attacked, refusing to defend them and himself on the basis that he's so pious, so self-righteous, that it would demean his personality if he fought back.

We know that the average Afro-American is not a pacifist. He's not a pacifist and he has never been a pacifist and he's not made of the type of material that would make a good pacifist. Those who doubt that the great majority of Negroes are not pacifists, just let them slap one. Pick any Negro on any street corner in the U.S.A. and they'll find out how much he believes in turning the other cheek.

All those who dare to attack are going to learn the hard way that the Afro-American is not a pacifist; that he cannot forever be counted on not to defend himself. Those who attack him brutally and ruthlessly can no longer expect to attack him with impunity.

The Afro-American cannot forget that his enslavement in this country did not pass because of pacifist moral force or noble appeals to the Christian conscience of the slaveholders.

Henry David Thoreau is idealized as an apostle of non-violence, the writer who influenced Gandhi, and through Gandhi, Martin Luther King, Jr. But Thoreau was not dogmatic; his eyes were open and he saw clearly. I keep with me a copy of Thoreau's *Plea For Captain John Brown*. There are truths that are just as evident in 1962 as they were in 1859 when he wrote:

> ". . . It was his [John Brown's] peculiar doctrine that a man has a perfect right to interfere by force with the slaveholder, in order to rescue the slave. I agree with him. They who are continually shocked by slavery have some right to be shocked by the violent death of the slaveholder, but such will be more shocked by his life than by his death. I shall not be forward to think him mistaken in his method who quickest succeeds to liberate the slave.
>
> "I speak for the slave when I say, that I prefer the philanthropy of Captain Brown to that philanthropy which neither shoots me nor liberates me. . . . I do not wish to kill nor to be killed, but I can foresee circumstances in which both these things would be by me unavoidable. We preserve the so-called peace of our community by deeds of petty violence every day.

Look at the policeman's billy and handcuffs! Look at the jail! . . . We are hoping only to live safely on the outskirts of this provisional army. So we defend ourselves and our hen-roosts, and maintain slavery. I know that the mass of my countrymen think that the only righteous use that can be made of Sharpe's rifles and revolvers is to fight duels with them, when we are insulted by other nations, or to hunt Indians, or shoot fugitive slaves with them or the like. I think that for once the Sharpe's rifles and the revolvers were employed in a righteous cause. The tools were in the hands of one who could use them.

"The same indignation that is said to have cleared the temple once will clear it again. The question is not about the weapon, but the spirit in which you use it. No man has appeared in America, as yet, who loved his fellowman so well, and treated him so tenderly. He [John Brown] lived for him. He took up his life and he laid it down for him. What sort of violence is that which is encouraged, not by soldiers, but by peaceable citizens, not so much by laymen as by ministers of the Gospel, not so much by the fighting sects as by the Quakers, and not so much by Quaker men as by Quaker women?

"This event advertises me that there is such a fact as death; the possibility of a man's dying. It seems as if no man had ever died in America before; for in order to die you must first have lived."

It is in the nature of the American Negro, the same as all other men, to fight and try to destroy those things that block his path to a greater happiness in life.

"The Future Belongs to Today's Oppressed"

Whenever I speak on the English-language radio station in Havana (which broadcasts for an audience in the United States) I hope in some way to penetrate the mental barriers and introduce new disturbing elements into the consciousness of white America. I hope to make them aware of the monstrous evil that they are party to by oppressing

123

the Negro. Somehow, I must manage to clearly reflect the image of evil that is inherent in a racist society so that white America will be able to honestly and fully see themselves as they really are. To see themselves with the same clarity as foreigners see them and to recognize that they are not champions of democracy. To understand that today they do not really even *believe* in democracy. To understand that the world is changing regardless of whether they *think* they like it or not.

For I know that if they had a glimpse of their own reality the shock would be of great therapeutic value. There would be many decent Americans who would then understand that this society must mend its ways if it is to survive; that there is no place in the world now for a racist nation.

As an individual, I'm not inclined toward "politics." The only thing I care about is justice and liberation. I don't belong to any political party. But I think that as long as the present politics prevails the Negro is not going to be integrated into American society. There will have to be great political changes before that can come about.

Those Americans who most deny the logic of the future are the ones who have driven me into exile. Those people have been cruel. Yet cruel as it may be, this exile was not the end those people had planned for me. But it is not in the hands of today's oppressors to determine my end. Their role in history denies to them an understanding of this, just as their role will not allow them to understand that every true nationalist leader in Africa has been imprisoned or exiled, and that the future leaders of Latin American and Asian national liberation today are experiencing imprisonment, exile, or worse.

The future belongs to today's oppressed and I shall be witness to that future in the liberation of the Afro-American.

The two sons of Robert F. Williams at each end. The boys in the middle are Joven Rebeldes, the Cuban Youth Organization (photo by LeRoy McLucas).

EPILOGUE

by Marc Schleifer

There is something about Robert F. Williams that frightens most American liberals—and many old-time radicals. Yet he is an attractive, interesting political figure to the many young people who have suddenly found themselves involved in politics in the last few years. I'm referring to the students who participate in peace demonstrations, the Freedom-Riders, the bohemians and artists who dug Fidel Castro in the Sierras and now defend his revolution. That social phenomenon which has taken a generalizing form from different responses—what C. Wright Mills referred to as the New Left. Why is Williams so attractive to the New Left and often somewhat distasteful to the Old one?

I think that both groups are responding to a sense of Williams' *radical insistence on immediacy*. The young Negro intellectuals entered the civil-rights struggle with a mentality expressing itself in the slogan—"Freedom Now!" The peace demonstrators are protesting the reasonable prospect of world-wide destruction some time this evening, or possibly tomorrow afternoon. The Beat Fidelistas were won over by the barbudos because of their almost hopelessly romantic struggle and the apocalyptic quality of their goals, in other words precisely because they were revolutionaries rather than politicians.

But Williams' insistence on immediacy rubs against the style of the Old Left. Perhaps this is an incorrect designation. I do not think Williams would have made Big Bill Haywood, Jack Reed, Gene Debs, or Jack London uncomfortable. And I know that he enjoys the respect of W. E. B. DuBois. Better the phrase, the Middle-Aged Left. One major historical event—the New Deal—separates Middle-Age experience from that of the truly Old and New Left.

Its first political commitment was linked to the optimism and the best aspirations of the New Deal, and I suggest that its sense of style has been shaped by the experience. The Middle-Aged Left knows, intellectually, that the New Deal is forever dead, but emotionally it cannot quite accept this as a fact, and it has never quite recovered from its sudden isolation from a world of respectability and authority that nourished it for years. It is a style that is summed by the word "progressive." As a point of style it is interesting to note that Williams never once uses the word "progressive" in this book. When I meet other young radicals and talk with them, I almost never encounter the word in their vocabulary. When I do, I inquire and invariably I am talking with someone from a leftist family or with political associations that pre-date the New Left. The young people of the New Left consider and openly label themselves as radicals or even revolutionaries.

But if we are to seriously consider this division of the American Left into categories-by-chronology we then have a case where (to misapply some theory) a quantitative change should not necessarily lead to a qualitative change. Think of Eugene Debs in Atlanta. There was nothing *old* about the Old American Left. For many of the Middle-Aged Left this is a description of an affliction, an emotional and intellectual sclerosis, but for those who have established lines of free communication with the New Left, it is solely a statistic of birthdate.

I had always intended but never got around to asking Robert Williams if he has ever read George Sorel's *Reflections on Violence*. I doubt it. But I throw in his name, which suggests an interesting parallel to some of Williams' ideas, for the sake of an academic strawman. Williams' sources are not European. His ideas are pure expressions of his social existence as a Southern Negro. Nor is his stand one that makes him a unique figure in Afro-American history. He is unique only in that sheltered white consciousness that never read of the slave revolts in its history textbooks, and knows exactly who Booker T. Washington is, but only vaguely if at all of W. E. B. DuBois.

Since the time of Reconstruction there have been Afro-Americans advocating much of the core of what Robert Williams advocates. Typical is the prominent Negro journalist John E. Bruce and his 1889 prophesy:

"I fully realize the delicacy of the position I occupy . . . and know too well that those who are to follow me will largely benefit by what I shall have to say in respect to the application of force as one of the means to the solution of the problem known as the Negro problem. I am not unmindful of the fact that there are those living who have faith in the efficacy of submission. . . . Those who are thus minded will advise a pacific policy in order as they believe to effect a settlement of this question, with which the statesmanship of a century has grappled without any particularly gratifying results. Agitation is a good thing, organization is a better thing. The million Negro voters of Georgia, and the undiscovered millions in other southern states—could with proper organization and intelligent leadership meet force with force with most beneficial results. . . .

"Under the present condition of affairs the only hope, the only salvation for the Negro is to be found in a resort to force under wise and discreet leaders. . . . The Negro must not be rash and indiscreet either in action or in words but he must be very determined and terribly in earnest, and of one mind to bring order out of chaos and to convince southern rowdies and cutthroats that more than two can play at the game with which they have amused their fellow conspirators in crime for nearly a quarter of a century.

"Organized resistance to organized resistance is the best remedy for the solution of the vexed problem of the century which to me seems practicable and feasible and I submit this view of the question, ladies and gentlemen, for your careful consideration."

128

ERRATA

A few ·corrections by Mr. Williams arrived too late for insertion in the text.

Page 42: Negroes are one quarter the population of Monroe, not one third.

Page 44: Williams was pushed one quarter of a mile, not one quarter of an hour.

Page 47: Steve Pressman should be Steve Presson.

Page 58 ff.: Sissy's last name is Sutton, not Marcus, and Sutton should be substituted for Marcus throughout.

Page 59: The English reporter was from the London *News Chronicle,* not the *Observer.*

Page 94: Albert Rurie should be Albert Rorie.

Page 95: Richard Griswald should be Richard Griswold.

gifts share

regenerate

re-learn A Lot

protocol

processes get 7 people

Voice

Agreement

Relearn

Voyage

Voyage

↓

Joy being together

RELEARN

Recommended Readings

- The Teachings of Ptahhotep: The Oldest Book in the World

- The Five Negro Presidents: According to what White People Said They Were

- 100 Amazing Facts About the Negro with Complete Proof: A Short Cut to The World History of The Negro

- From Babylon to Timbuktu: A History of the Ancient Black Races Including the Black Hebrews

Available at www.bnpublishing.com

My Bubble ←

① What brings liberals out?   cover

→ CANNABIS CARAVANS — type of protest

why do you like something

Page Break

Playful

Joke   >   ⊕ What Am i doing there?
                        — wide ocean & —

Morality   (the other)   → Avenues of thinking

                              Economic SEX

Ship De EMBARK   PATRIARCHY

                                        gender SEX

individual   Sinach   Return to the
                            Source
               Mayan house

   ↑   Sami   BINA~
Counter insurgency

←↔   (Anything different) [Not Answer to curses]   Perpetrator

put us in Competition → WORK →   Victim

                     Working Together

              ↓   ↓ MALE femme   Competition
                  SHARE

How do   Communar   class   Strike
we get to   RACE   ↳ SHARING
that port?   Auditor

Make create   Process to choose!
Collective Agreements

                    who
                           —Destiny   Situated
Many Worlds   Distance from Source   Collectiy
                                         Use to
Other Seperation   Binaries.   engage the Tour

                        / individual is the indivl

B the inc

CPSIA information can be obtained
at www.ICGtesting.com
Printed in the USA
FSHW011314250221
78949FS

Are we our worst counter insurgei

If so how do
find that Space of the other?